Acknowledgements

Everything you read in these pages was first heard by a group of listeners somewhere. Most of those listeners were parishioners, while the "somewhere" in question was most likely a sanctuary. By actual count, I have preached in eight countries and seventeen states. I have preached with and without translators, with and without pulpits and with and without systems of amplification. But the great majority of my years were clustered in four United Methodist congregations in Michigan, all within twenty miles of each other. By name they were First UMC (Dearborn), Newburg UMC (Livonia), Nardin Park UMC (Farmington Hills), and First UMC (Birmingham). Those congregations took me in, heard me out, and prayed me up, which means that I was both encouraged and critiqued by friends. Week after week they turned monologues into dialogues. Little did they know how much they kept me going.

But to get these words into print required transcription and word processing expertise, which explains my special appreciation to Karen DeBenedet, Judy Hood, Audrey Mangum, Debbie Prasad, Janet Smylie and Ginny Young.

But the persons who most wanted this to happen were my wife, Kristine, my daughter, Julie Hopkins, and my editorial collaborator, Lindsay Hinz. Without them I would not have gotten around to it, or gotten through it. They could see the finish line and knew how to get there. Otherwise, tomorrow would have stretched into eternity.

Preface

For the first three years of my ministry, I had the privilege of serving as an associate pastor for Bill at Birmingham First United Methodist. I liken those years to a young ball player being able to watch Ted Williams take batting practice. Like Williams, Ritter is master at his craft. He has studied it. Worked hard to perfect it. Has command of it. Knows the importance of it. Seems to be able to place the message wherever it needs to be placed. And when it matters most, there is no one you want taking a swing in the pulpit but him.

I was thrilled when Bill asked me to take a look at *Preaching in the Key of Life*. It was so refreshing to experience his messages again. It was almost like drinking a smooth, dark porter on cold winter's night. Bill's words did what they have always done for me, they filled me up with warmth that started in center of my chest and spread comfort across my whole being. By the time I had savored the last drop I simply felt better about myself, my faith, and my world.

These sermons felt awful familiar. They didn't feel familiar just because I had heard Dr. Ritter preach (seven of them). They felt familiar because Bill's writing and preaching has a way of gently cracking us open. His turning of a phrase peels back our defenses, cynicisms and anxieties, while his stories often feel like he has discovered one our old love letters or stumbled across the missing page from our diary. In his sermon's, Bill always seemed to know us.

Bill's preaching never comes from a place above us but instead he always lets us know that he is walking right alongside us. He puts himself into the sermons he preaches. Both moments of deep joy and unbelievable sadness are found in these pages. Nor is Bill afraid to honor our doubts, because they are his doubts too. And most importantly, Bill introduces us over and over to the God who in Christ meets us in the midst of the very real lives we lead.

There has been much written about the decline of the United Methodist Church. Preaching in the Key of Life is a reminder that much our revival will come from the pulpit. Preaching is our moment to rally the congregation for mission, to remind people they are loved beyond measure, to help folks wrestle with tough issues and to remind them that forgiveness and grace are always available. And when done well, and Bill does this as well as anyone, the sermon can cast a vision for a church that might actually change the world. All I can say is that these "will preach!" And they have!

Rev. Jeff Nelson
Senior Pastor, First United Methodist Church
Royal Oak, Michigan

Table of Contents

Foreword

This guy. Writing. On a Saturday. Potentially one of the most vivid memories of my youth. A black felt tip pen, legal size white paper. Rich thoughts. Woven together into thought provoking, sometimes life changing prose. When anyone compliments my writing, and even hints that it resembles his, they don't know how intensely I take it as a compliment. But as Dan Fogelberg aptly summarized, "my life has been a poor attempt to imitate the man."

He is a marvelous writer, but also so much more, a fact which I found myself pondering on Fathers Day, as book production was in full force. Because it struck me that 2017 marked the 50th anniversary of his first Father's Day, as my brother would have turned 50 the week prior. Would have, of course, because he's been gone since 1993. But here we have remained. And in many ways, as a family, we have landed stronger.

Why? Because he (in strong, committed partnership with my mom) showed us how. He struggled and persevered through life's messiest and most difficult stuff – and he talked us through it – through conversations in our house, in our community, from the pulpit – and taught us all how to persevere. A great writer, he is. But his words were more than prose, they were leadership, and in dark moments, light.

Through our dark days, he spoke of and showed resilience. Those sermons have been the one that have carried so many through similar, or even just equally painful, valleys. But his leadership didn't end there. It has also been the companion to many of life's other pivots, peaks and pauses. For this reason, these, and other sermons have been travelling person to person, for years.

Some of the most popular and relevant texts are shared in the pages that follow. But among the words that I have passed along over time, and in truth have probably even copped as my own, are the following:

"Life is full of jungles, which can be anywhere, can't they? And life is also full of predators, who can be anybody, can't they? Sometimes the "devouring" is an inside job, as in the question, "what's eating you, my

friend?" Having lived in city and suburb, I have seen people eaten in both places. Having worked in both among poor and rich, I have seen people eaten in both circumstances. Whether it be war and violence, depression and disillusionment, poverty and peer envy, or sickness and bereavement, no one walks the road of life without encountering some hungry lions.

And these lions will pounce. And maim. And cripple. For that is the nature of lions. That is what lions do. If they don't take your life, they will take their toll. Do not, for a minute, make light of that. For after meeting a lion, you will never be the same. Some people go through a crisis and say, "I've got to get back to my old self." But that's a fruitless quest. You will never get back to your "old self." For the crisis has taken your "old self" with it. You'll never get it back. Ever.

But that doesn't mean you can't come out with something. For one of the strangest, yet most sublime facts of human existence is that something beneficial can often be harvested from life's most devastating experiences.

Because lessons learned, if internalized, may turn out to be honey in the lion. History offers us story after story in illustration of my point, people who found something to eat in the thing that was eating them. And I've got to believe that many of you have made a return trip down the old road where the lion lay, and may still lie, and have taken your fistful of honey from his gut, however many years may have passed in the meantime."

••••••••

Dad, you have seen, processed, and shared so much. Your words, like lyrics, have been part of much of what guides many of our days. And with this publishing, they are bound to guide many more.

You have been through the jungle, but I believe what we have recaptured as a family, over almost 25 years, counts as sweet sweet honey. And at this point in your life, I hope you are enjoying a sticky handful.

Julie Ritter Hopkins
Northville, MI
Father's Day, 2017

Introduction

In a 3000-member congregation, Jack Baker could have easily gotten lost. For while Jack and Susie attended regularly and supported the church generously, my relationship with them was more casual than close. As a famous pediatric eye surgeon at Children's Hospital in Detroit, Jack's hands were as full as they were talented. Whenever our paths crossed, he invariably said nice things to me. And from feedback gleaned from others, I gathered he also said nice things about me. Ours was an easy familiarity, though not necessarily a deep one.

After twelve years as his pastor (and forty years "doing time" in United Methodist pulpits), I retired from local church ministry and accepted an invitation to teach preaching to seminarians at Duke Divinity School. But retaining a primary residence in Michigan, I still functioned pastorally when invited to do so. I took on a few "Interims" when the bishop asked, filled a few pulpits when a pastor asked, officiated at a few funerals when a family asked, and consecrated a few weddings when a bride asked. Which is how it came to pass that I was in South Lyon, MI one sweet summer Saturday to help tie a marital knot for Nora King and Stu Baker. Both were well seasoned in life experience. And both were happy to be undertaking this new adventure.

Dr. Jack Baker is the groom's uncle. But having forgotten that connection, it was a pleasant serendipity to see my former parishioner in the congregation. When the wedding was over, Jack hung back during the meet and greet time. Then, approaching me directly, he asked if there was a place we could speak privately. Finding the host pastors office empty, we commandeered it, and Jack shut the door. I was a little apprehensive, more for Jack than for me. Was it something about Susie … or family … about his own health … or his work at the hospital? It turned out to be none of the above. What he wanted to do was thank me for my ministry and tell me what I had meant to him. "I've missed you," he said. "More than you know," he added. "Your sermons were so personal, so important, so riveting," he continued. And then, struggling to find just the right words, he concluded: "I don't know if this is the right way to say it, but it's the best way I know. You preach life. I hope I haven't said anything wrong. But you preach life."

I understood what he meant. Simply put, he could see himself in my sermons. Which may have been because he could see me in my sermons. There was a transparency that was illuminating. All of which makes preachers nervous. And which makes almost all teachers of preachers nervous. "Remember" we were told by our Homiletics professors, "it's not about you." We were told to filter the messenger out of the message. Let the Gospel speak with its own voice and impact the listener with its own power. The Bible throbs with all the life it will ever need. Read it. Feel it. Preach it. But don't get in its way.

Which, at the outset, I took seriously. But then I ran into people like Phillips Brooks and P.T. Forsyth who defined preaching thusly: "Preaching is the communication of truth through personality." Which not only made room for me but asked a great deal of me. On the one hand, this includes the illustrations I select, the applications I suggest, and the quotes I choose to buttress my argument. I go through life seeing movies, reading books, holding conversations, and eavesdropping on everyday events. Which leads me to say (twenty or thirty times a week), "that'll preach." And then I look for an opportunity to slot such moments into sermons.

But what about my personal life experiences? I am talking about self-revelation. It goes without saying that good preachers need to be clear about their text. But good preachers need not hide behind their text. Meaning that good preaching is sometimes self–exposing. When you take a Dale Carnegie course in public speaking, you are told to conquer your fear of the audience by picturing them naked. But what they never tell you in seminary is that one of the things that can help a sermon "connect" is when the congregation is permitted to see the preacher naked. Transparency is often a very helpful step on the road to authenticity. If I have heard it once, I have heard it (literally) a hundred times in my ministry: "Thanks for sharing so honestly and personally with us." Which I have done, not accidentally but intentionally.

So is this legitimate? I trust so. So does one of my preaching heroes, the late William Sloane Coffin, who wrote: "Finally you preach for yourself. But if you go down deep enough, you touch enough common humanity so that everyone is involved."

Which means that shallow sharing won't do the job. You don't do vacation summaries or family travelogues. And you keep in mind that at least half the congregation has grandchildren who do and say exceedingly clever things. Yours are not unique. On the flip side, however, you don't do self-therapy in the pulpit, nor do you expose personal wounds that are still too raw for public viewing. What's more, you do not repeatedly tell stories which paint you as the hero or stories which are consistently self-deprecating. And it goes without saying that you should never embarrass your spouse, your children or an unsuspecting parishioner.

Instead, what you do is listen to life as it is being lived within and around you, Then you report what you hear so that you can relate what you hear to the text before you and the people around you. One of the more career enhancing maladies from which a preacher can suffer is Attention Surplus Disorder. I feel no need to defend myself against the charge that I have been mis-focused. Forty years worth of parishioners have rendered their own judgment, and I am content to live with it. One of those listeners is, of course, me. What you are about to read are a number of sermons I needed to preach because at the moment I preached them, they were sermons I needed to hear. But in preaching them, they hopefully became sermons other people needed to hear. Because they told me so. For everyone who said, "I know a little bit more about you because I heard you preach," the comments I treasured most came from those who said, " I think I know a little bit more about myself because I heard you preach." Just a few weeks ago one of them wrote, "You were a mentor and an inspiration to me. My husband and I never knew when we'd be in the next Sunday's sermon." But let the record show that never once in 12 years did I expose the writer or her husband or slip any of their stories into my manuscript.

Did any of this lead to a deepening of faith? God, I hope so. All I know is that people said it did. My faculty colleague at Duke, Dr. Richard Lischer, writes: "In a culture brimming with stories, we have somehow mislaid the beauty and drama of the narratives that belong to us, or to which we belong. Writing is like confessing, except that it's harder, more exposed, and almost never followed by absolution. But when joined to the traditional practices of preaching, sacrament, and catechesis, the telling of a life helps shape Christian identity and discipleship."

Hopefully, it led my parishioners to say (with apologies to "When Harry Met Sally"), "I'll have what he's having." After all, would I really love to tell the story if it hadn't already done so much for me?

What follows are 20 sermons preached over a 30-year period. Unfortunately, you are being asked to read them. I did not write them to be read. I wrote them to be heard. And I have not reconstructed them for the eye instead of the ear. That's because most of you can hear between the lines.

So are these my best sermons? That depends on where you stand or sit when you read them. If you are an academician with a Ph.D. in Homiletics, hardly. If you are among the religiously curious looking to gain a little insight into the will and ways of God, possibly. And if you are a pew sitter who has dragged body and baggage into church looking for something that will challenge, comfort or get you through another week, hopefully. But, speaking personally, I will be pleased with an interested audience of two.

I am talking about my grandchildren who, at this writing, are ages ten and eight. To them, I am not Rev. Ritter. I am not Pastor Bill. Nor am I Brother Billy. To them, I am "Boppa," married to "Neena." And the best way I can tell them a little of my story is in the context of a much bigger story. To whatever degree they will learn about God and Jesus in the process of learning a little about me, I will be happy.

So, Jacob Ritter Hopkins and Georgia Grace Hopkins, these sermons are for you.

William Ritter
Northville, Michigan
2017

Georgia Grace Hopkins and Jacob Ritter Hopkins, 2017

1

Connecting The Dots

On a cold winter's day over lunch at my favorite Chinese restaurant, Rev. Gary Haller invited me to be the guest speaker for a first-ever Legacy Dinner for Birmingham First United Methodist Church on a Friday night in May. Sponsored by the Endowment Committee, its goal was to raise consciousness and promote planned giving for the church's Endowment Fund. But Gary told me I didn't have to talk about money, which was something of a relief given that I had spent twelve years, from 1993 to 2005, with my hand in these people's pockets. "Just talk about your ministry, your life, or even what you have been doing since you left Birmingham. It doesn't have to be a sermon. Let's call it a reflection."

On Friday evening, May 6 of 2016, I made good on my commitment. A few months later, my heart doctors at the University of Michigan asked what I was doing around 7:30 or 8:00 p.m. on Friday, May 6. It seems that an implanted recorder in my chest had detected several abnormalities and irregularities traceable to those 30 minutes. Instantly, I remembered what I had been doing on that night at that locale. So whatever else can be said about what you are about to read, no one can complain that my heart wasn't in it. Especially my cardiologist.

A Vocational Reflection

Kindly allow me to return you to your early childhood. You were three or maybe four years old when you first saw one. I am talking about those children's activity books that included multiple pages where you were invited to complete a picture by connecting the dots. The page itself was filled with tiny dots. They were oddly spaced. And there was a barely discernible number beside each dot. Your job was to connect the dots by moving your pencil sequentially through the numbers until something recognizable came into view. But the dots (and their numbers) were not always where you thought they were going to be (like right next to the dot you just left).

This little exercise tested you on three levels.

1. Could you make straight lines with your pencil (which was a precursor to another lesson ... a lifelong lesson ... testing whether you could color inside the lines)?

2. Did you know your numbers by sequence? You had to know

that 11 followed 10 or that 20 followed 19, or you were doomed before you started.

3. Did you have enough visual imagination to figure out what you were drawing before you got to the end of the numbers and connected all of the dots? At what point could you look at a work-in-progress and say, "This is going to be a house … or a horse … or an elephant … or the East Garden of the Palace of Versailles"? At what point could you jump from what was there to be seen to what was as yet unseen?

Ah, if only we had more pastors who could not only see what all of us see, but who could see something else, something better, and something in the future. Such a pastor could take us to the next dot, to the one after that, and to the one after the one after that. That pastor could then help us see a vision, and maybe even catch it.

Do we have many of those pastors? Unfortunately, no. Most pastors can see what's there. And most pastors can serve what's there. But any more than that, good luck.

This works for most congregations. Because they, too, can see what's already there. And even more congregations can see what used to be there. But most have a hard time visualizing the future.

Many of our churches say "Send us a pastor who can take us to the next level." But you have to be able to see the next level. It's called pastoral imagination. But very few seminary professors teach it. Because very few teachers of preachers have it.

But when you're a kid, it's easy. If you know your numbers and are adept with a pencil, you just take your pencil and begin to draw. But when there are no more visible numbers (and your picture doesn't seem to be finished), it's harder. Kindly allow me to illustrate, both personally and professionally.

There may have been a road for me marked "Ministry," but either it was not well marked or I was too blind to see it at the time. Which is why I am now going back in my mind to see how I got here. Was God in it from the beginning? Quite possibly. But only now, as I connect my dots in reverse, am I seeing what should have been obvious earlier. Except it wasn't. No, not obvious at all.

As some of you know, I am married to a crackerjack genealogist. Which explains why we watch shows like "Who Do You Think You Are" and "Finding Your Roots." The latter of those shows features the brilliant Harvard researcher Henry Louis Gates Jr., who is the best cure for insomnia that television ever offered. But it was because of Henry Louis Gates that Kris and I spit saliva into individual tubes and sent them to Ancestry.com to learn our biological DNA. Hers was all over the map, including trace elements from Northern Africa, Polynesia, and even Russia. I had no surprises. Over 75% of my ancestry traces to

Eastern Europe and Ireland. The name "Ritter" is German. Only 7% of my bloodline can be traced to Germany. But the Germans in my family tree were probably Protestants. While my Eastern European relatives (Slovenian) and my Irish ancestors literally screamed "Roman Catholic."

This is how it played out in the generations closest to me. Three of my four grandparents were Roman Catholic. But only one (my father's father) was Protestant. Not that it mattered much. All anybody in my family knew was what church they were staying away from. People often ask me if I come from a long line of preachers. Heck, I don't come from a long line of churchgoers. My parents were married by a Methodist minister because his church was in my father's boyhood neighborhood and my father remembered going there once (as a child) because they gave him popcorn. And when that minister agreed to officiate at my parents' wedding, he dictated that it be done at his parsonage. The assumption was that he couldn't marry them in the church because they had no connection to the church.

No, my people were not religious people. Neither were they materially well-off people. My father was a custodian for the Detroit Public Library system, and he customarily worked a second job to make ends meet. My mother worked as a salesperson at the downtown Detroit J.L. Hudson store, eventually becoming a full-time executive secretary when my father was involuntarily retired in his mid-forties on a disability pension. His affliction was brittle diabetes complicated by alcoholism. But I don't remember feeling poor, although I certainly don't remember feeling flush.

Neither cupboard nor closet was bare. But there were few extras. Life was fairly simple. I didn't hunt, fish, golf or ski. Nor did I know anybody who did such things. I had good male friends (three Catholics and a Jew). I played baseball at the schoolyard, touch football on a vacant lot, hockey in the street, and basketball in the alley (shooting at a hoop attached to Bill Bowman's garage). I also played the violin, taking private lessons for seven or eight years. I was better off than many teenagers because I had a big paper route. I delivered the Detroit News seven days a week and 365 days a year. As for girls, I don't remember having much time for them. But as a kid with an all-consuming paper route who played the violin, I wouldn't exactly call myself a "chick magnet."

But I went to church. A lot. I'm talking about the same church where the minister had once agreed to marry my mother and father. He also "christened" me. That's the Roman Catholic word for what most of us now call baptism.

My parents took me to church. Thankfully, it was just down the block. In the early years, they dropped me off. Then they came back and picked me up. Eventually my mother got involved, joining the church on the same day I was confirmed as a sixth grader. My father came sporadically, sat in the balcony, and never became a member formally. But because the church was close … and because the church was kind … and maybe because the church created a climate of comfort and consistency that I did not always experience at home, I spent a lot of time there. I attended Sunday school, Vacation Bible School, and the youth group. I sang in the choir at every age level. And since our church had a gym, I played on church basketball teams … in a league … with uniforms … and trophies. Because my church sponsored all levels of scouting, I was a Cub Scout, Boy Scout, and Explorer Scout. I also went on campouts. But every summer I also went to a church camp. I did this for eight consecutive summers. Eventually, some other pastors got to know me, and I became a district youth officer and an Annual Conference youth officer. As a senior in high school, I was invited to become a youth lay delegate to Annual Conference.

And every Sunday, I went to worship. I was an acolyte. I carried flags. And finally, the cross. For God's sake, I carried that big, heavy cross down the aisle, leading the choir. At least I assumed I was doing it "for God's sake."

I was a church junkie, don't you see. And ordinary lay people don't know what to do when they see the same kid in church every time they turn around. They figure that he must be one of those odd ones…not "odd" as in "weird," but "odd" as in "special." So people began asking me if the church was going to be my life's work. And older women with blue rinse in their hair began patting me on the head and saying,

"I'll just bet you're going to be a minister someday." And I thought, "Why not," "Maybe they're right," "This might not be the world's dumbest idea."

So I began trying the idea on. After all, I liked the place. I liked the people. I liked the work (what little I knew of it). And I suppose I liked being liked. It's nice to be liked. So much so, that I began to express an interest in ministry. Even more so when it came to thinking about higher education, and my minister said, "That boy is going to Albion."

Now having earlier heard me say that my people were not religious people, you should also know that my people were not broadly educated people. I never doubted that they were bright. But nobody in my family had ever been to college. One semester before my father's high school graduation, he hopped a freight train with Louis Malchie for California. He said he wanted to see the world. But maybe what he really wanted was to avoid the world. My friends in the neighborhood didn't talk about college. Nor did they visit any. As for me, there was no dot in my picture for college. Where was Albion? I didn't know. What was Albion? I didn't know. How was anybody going to pay for Albion? I didn't know. But it seemed right.

After all, I'd had an eleventh grade English teacher in high school who said, "Mr. Ritter, I see bigger things in store for you." And I had a high school principal who called me down to his office to say, "Mr. Ritter, your grades are decent, but if you were to click things into a higher gear for the next couple of semesters, I might be able to do something for you." So I did, and he did. I got scholarship money. But I didn't know that most of it came from Paul and Ethel Halmhuber, who were members of my boyhood church. And it was only forty years later that I learned that they were the great-grandparents of Scott Chrostek.

I saw Albion for the first time on the day I moved my stuff into the dorm. And while the college catalog had a four-year class selection plan for pre-ministerial students (the very plan I had signed up for), I remember thinking to myself on my last night at home: "If I can just complete one year, I will have gone further than anybody in my family has ever gone, and I will feel successful."

Well, things worked out. I got a job waiting tables. And given that I was a pretty good tenor, I got into the choir. And made some friends. I survived freshman chemistry. And I was asked to join a fraternity. I don't know what got into me, but I said, "As ridiculous, frivolous and irresponsible as a fraternity seems, I think I need this." So I became a T.K.E. Summers, I got good jobs. These included four summers as a tour guide at the Ford Motor Company. Every day I wore a company suit and led people through the Rouge plant. That's where I got rid of any fear I might have had about talking to strangers over a microphone. Every other kid who got a similar job was the son of an upper-level Ford executive. Most of my summer colleagues had fathers who were vice presidents. How did I get my job? It came via a recommendation from a Ford guy at my church.

Are you seeing a pattern here? My church paved my way into ministry. My church opened doors for me into ministry. And my church pushed me through those doors into ministry.

There were no burning bushes (Moses), no smoke-filled epiphanies in the Temple (Isaiah), no blindsided muggings on the road to Damascus (Paul), and not even any still, small voices beside the lakeshore (hymn 349). I never wrestled with God. I never fought God. But one night, in a very quiet and almost forgettable way, I surrendered and said "Uncle" to God.

Heck, my church called me into ministry. I am talking about all those wonderful people at my church in the city which breathed its last in 1977. Among those people at my church were Cliff and Isabel Bath who were my Sunday school teachers before they were even married. And there was Bob Ward, who was my youth minister before he was even married.

For years I felt grateful to my church. But I also felt guilty that, as calls to ministry go, mine wasn't all that dramatic. There was nothing all that decisive. Neither was there anything all that divine. Until one day, years later, I realized that God is sneaky sometimes, putting the bite on people like me through dear, sweet old ladies with blue rinse in their hair.

Meanwhile, my little world (my confining cocoon) was expanding as I plowed on toward divinity school. Six months before my graduation from Albion, one of my professors asked me where I was going to seminary. I gave him my two options. Both of them were Methodist. Both of them were Midwestern. Both of them were as safe and comfortable as they were obvious. But then he said, "No, you're not. You're going to Yale or Harvard." I thought it was the dumbest thing anybody had ever said to me. People like me don't go to schools like that. But he wouldn't lay it to rest. Every day he brought it up. Finally I applied to Yale and Harvard just to shut him up. I pictured the admissions committees at those schools laughing uproariously at the pretention of my application. But the last laugh belonged to my Albion professor. It came when I was admitted and funded at both Yale and Harvard.

Scared to death, I chose Yale. I had my first mind blowing experience the next Friday when the Episcopalians had a cocktail party on the quadrangle. "Billy," (I said), "this isn't Kansas anymore." But I got good grades and a pair of good field work jobs in ministry. I worked for two years in a suburban Methodist church on the Gold Coast (between New Haven and New York). And I worked the third year in the worst ghetto in New Haven. What I found out was that, as far as ministry goes, I could not only study it but do it. And halfway through my Yale experience, I realized (in the words of the late Frank Sinatra) that "If I can make it here, I'll make it anywhere."

And I suppose it was that realization that put Birmingham into the picture. As a kid growing up in Detroit, I was never in Birmingham … even once. That is until my Albion College choir sang here one night as part of its spring tour. I don't remember a thing about it. But somebody introduced me to the minister. He was a big man, as I remember … a little bit gruff, as I remember … with a name I remembered. Arnold Runkel, it was. And though I've forgotten everything else about that evening, I remembered that name. Another dot, don't you see.

Then there was my first district superintendent, the late Herb Hausser. The year before I came back from Yale, I told him I just wanted a couple of small churches where I could preach every Sunday. I expected to be shipped to mid-Michigan, or maybe even the Upper Peninsula. I told him the one thing I didn't want to do was be an associate pastor in a big church. So Herb sent me to Dearborn First as the fourth pastor on a staff of four. The church was huge. And when I arrived, it seemed like the Ford Motor Company at prayer. But I'll never forget his explanation for my placement. "I see you as someone who will one day be able to serve any church in the Conference, and I need to expose you, from day one, to the kind of congregation into which you will one day be placed." Ironically, it was in Dearborn that I played church league basketball with Ed Hagenlocker who, 35 years later (accompanied by his wife, Sylvia) would take Kris and me to dinner at the Ocean Grille and say, "If you have any desire to get serious about expanding First Church's building for youth and recreational ministry, Sylvia and I will write a seven figure check to start things off. In addition, we will pay the architectural fees for any and all conceptual drawings." We're talking a big dot ... big time.

Ed Hagenlocker shooting the first basket at the new Christian Life Center
at FUMC Birmingham.

Now, you just heard me mention Kris. I was 23 when we met. I had one more year at Yale to finish. She was 17 when we met. It was one month after her graduation from high school. I was serving as a vacation fill-in in Novi for four Sundays. The pastor who was leaving for California was none other than LaVere Webster (another dot). On the third Sunday of July, I was in the Novi pulpit. Kris was in the third pew. And my life has never been the same since. Fifty years ago, this July 2nd, she said, "I'll go with you on this wild and crazy ride." Although she never knew at that time that she'd have to do much of the steering. Dot. Dot. Dot. Bingo.

People have asked me if we ever expected to end up in Birmingham. Not really. We knew the possibility. But we were not without reservations. Frankly, we wondered whether we would be a good fit for the culture. But in 1992 I was asked by Bishop Judy Craig to lead a $6 million campaign for the denomination. I was at Nardin Park United Methodist Church at the time. Anticipating my reservations, she told me I would have a co-chair…a layman named Jay Hook…from First Church, Birmingham. For two years Jay and I were linked at the hip, traveling the state and pitching a program. During the same two years, Jay was linked maritally with Joan. And during those same two years, Joan was on First Church's Staff Parish Relations Committee, chaired by Dale Parker. And during those same two years, Bob Ward was moving toward retirement. We're talking more dots about to be connected.

Do I believe in divine design? Not in the way the Calvinists do. I have never believed that our lives are planned out and fore-ordained (what some would call Presbyterian Predestinationalism). No, as a character in Robert Penn Warren's classic novel, *All The Kings Men*, proclaims at the end of the book: "I've gotta believe it could have all been different."

Nothing in my background ever suggested I should have become your pastor. But as I look back on everything that has happened, I have to believe, if not in a doctrine of divine design, at least in the possibility of divine steerage (allowing for a lot of play in the wheel). And as concerns my ministry, while I still wrestle with the question of whether God has called me to it, I have grown quietly confident that God has used me in it.

And maybe still does. The other day my grandson, Jacob, with more seriousness than many nine-year-olds can muster, asked, "Boppa, how come you don't preach anymore?" Well, I do. Occasionally. But if retirement has three distinct phases (go-go, slow-go, and no-go), I am more or less sliding into slow-go. But hey, in the midst of writing this, just yesterday, I talked with a woman in Wrightsville Beach in North Carolina facing life-threatening heart surgery, a banker in Bloomfield whose stepson killed himself in a dorm room in Indiana, a woman in Livonia who I last pastored 36 years ago and who (with good reason) is really angry with God, and a very well-known local television personality who is wrestling with a new career possibility as a United Methodist pastor.

And then there's the delightful stuff. A few days ago I had a telephone call from Eleanor Chambliss. Eleanor was our lay leader, a

Trustee chair, and a co-chair to raise $6.5 million for the Christian Life Center. She also was, and still is, Sue Ives' mother. Today, she's a South Carolinian. She lives just outside of Charleston, where she is now an Episcopalian. (Editor's note: Eleanor Chambliss has recently moved home to Birmingham.) We talk a couple of times a year. She may call me. I may call her. This time we were on her dime. "I don't need anything special," she said. "But all day long I thought it would be nice to hear your voice. I used to feel the same way about Dr. Thomas and his voice. Of course, he's gone now." Which he is. G. Ernest Thomas concluded his ministry 22 years before I arrived here to begin mine. So what was Eleanor doing? Connecting some dots. That's what Eleanor was doing.

The late John Dunne once wrote, "I date my life from the beginning of my ministry." If I had read that at age 30…maybe even at age 40…I would have thought it ridiculous. But now, at 75, I both understand and pretty much agree. Because as the years slid by, I began to realize that who I was and what I did for a living had become indistinguishable, one from the other. "Minister" is who I am. Maybe, even who I have always been.

As for heaven, I'd just as soon trust it. But I am willing to wait for it. I recall the old Baptist preacher who screamed: "How many of you want to go to heaven?" Everybody in the congregation raised their hand but one. So the preacher shouted the question a second time. Same lone holdout. Finally the preacher left the pulpit, walked down the center aisle and stopped beside the man's pew. "Don't you want to go to heaven when you die?" he thundered. To which came back the answer, "Of course I want to go to heaven when I die. I just thought you was getting up a bus to go right now."

All things considered, I'll wait for a later bus.

First United Methodist Church
Birmingham, Michigan
May 6, 2016

2

A Little Night Fishing

Scripture: John 21:1-8

Seeking to acknowledge whatever anxiety might be present in the congregation the very first time that I stepped into the pulpit to begin my 12-year ministry in Birmingham, this sermon represented my attempt to address my own anxiety in language as biblical as it was revealing.

Once upon a time, there was an eager young seminarian who submitted a neatly typed sermon to his preaching professor for grading. When all the student-sermons were returned, this one carried the simple notation: "Grade pending. See me for consultation."

On the appointed day of the conference, the professor started out quite positively:

I like the way you handled the text. You did not misread the scripture. Neither did you twist it to suit your prejudices. What's more, your three points made sense. They showed balance and progression. Your introduction and conclusion evidenced no small amount of creativity. And your illustrations, while sometimes forced, set off your major points quite nicely. All things considered, I have decided to give you a D+.

The seminarian was clearly taken aback. "Why give me a D+," he cried, "if my sermon has as many things going for it as you claim?"

"Frankly," said the professor, "it's because of your title. It may be one of the worst titles I have ever seen. Nobody would come to hear a sermon entitled: 'The Narratives of Jesus' Resurrection in the Synoptic Gospels, as Considered in the Light of the Eschatology of the Apostle Paul.' But I'll tell you what I'll do. You come up with a better title, and I'll come up with a better grade. What you want is a title that will reach out and touch people ... one that will compel them to come in and hear what it is you have to say. Try to imagine your title on a sign in front of the church, having such an impact, that if a bus should stop in front of your church (however briefly), and if the people on that bus should see the sign (however fleetingly), your title would be so powerful that it would motivate them to get off the bus and march immediately into the sanctuary."

"So the seminarian went home, gave it his best shot, and returned the next morning to the professor's office. Same text. Brand new title. The sermon was now called: "Your Bus Has a Bomb on It."

My friends, if there was ever a morning I wanted to preach explosively ... if there was ever a morning I wanted to bond rather than bomb ... if there was ever a morning for coaxing you off the bus of complacency into the intricate work of ministry ... this is that morning. For I have poured so much thought, prayer and bottled energy into this day. I want to do well. I want us to do well. And I want whatever work God is going to entrust to our collective hands to do well. For I've got to tell you, I've been thinking about this day since the second Wednesday in February. That's when District Superintendent Phylemon Titus sat in our living room, looked at Kris and me, mentioned the name of this church, and said, "Let me tell you what Bishop Ott has in mind."

Now it's come down to this. And I'm nervous, I'll admit it. Because, unless I admit it, you won't know it. I'll hide it well. But I can't fool myself. My dreams give me away. In recent weeks I have started having fresh variations on an old dream theme ... one that has been with me for better than 25 years. I'll call it my "Unpreparedness Dream." Everybody dreams it in some form. The most universal form of the dream finds you back in high school or college. You are looking for one of your classes. But you can't find the room in which it is being taught. Or you can't find your books. Or you didn't bring a pencil. Or

31

you didn't finish your homework. Or you show up, not having attended the class in ages, only to discover that this is the day of the final exam. But the high school version of the dream is only one of its many manifestations. There are others. Take your pick. Fill in your own blanks. Then tell me later.

My personal version of the "Unpreparedness Dream" customarily involves preaching. When the time to preach comes, I am not ready. I am out in the narthex. The choir is all lined up. I can speak to them. I can see their faces. There they are ... robed and ready ... books in their hands. People are streaming into the sanctuary. Others are standing to sing. And I am there alongside them. But I am in a sweatshirt. Or I've forgotten my tie. Or my robe. Every now and again in this dream, I don't have any shoes. And I'll look at my watch and think to myself: "I wonder if I have time to go home and get dressed?"

Other times (in my dream) I am dressed. But I can't find the sermon. I wrote it. But I lost it. I left it somewhere and can't, for the life of me, remember where.

On other occasions, I've got it all (suit ... tie ... shoes ... socks ... sermon ... robe). But I can't find the church. One time it was the sanctuary I couldn't find. I was wandering all over the building ... down this corridor ... up that stairway ... running into one locked door after the other. I could hear the organ playing the hymn that I had specifically chosen to precede the sermon. I could hear the congregation singing the fourth (and final) verse. But I couldn't get to where the music was.

In the worst manifestation of the dream, the problem is not with my readiness, but with your receptivity. I've got my sermon. I'm dressed to the nines. I find the sanctuary. I get up to preach. And you're not there. You were there. But you had to go home early. You couldn't stay. While streaming past me on the way out the door, one or two of you tell me that I shouldn't take it personally. It's just that you are busy people with important things to do. But I do take it personally. Because your departure constitutes a painful extension of my dream theme. The first form of the dream plays into my fear of not being ready. But the second form of the dream plays into my fear of being ready but rejected.

That's powerful stuff. I know I am taking a risk in telling it to you. Except that I know something else which makes my revelation safer. I know that some of you are nervous too. You wonder what is going to happen ... how things are going to be ... how you are going to feel ... what I am going to say. Some of you are worried that everything that's been said about me won't be true. Others of you are worried that it will. Some of you are sizing matters up (even now), asking yourselves, "Does this sound like someone who will listen to us as well as lead us?" Meanwhile, others of you are pondering things more personal still, asking, "Does this sound like someone we can eventually trust to marry us ... or bury us?"

And all the while you are wondering what I am thinking of you. In this four-month transition of occasional conversations and comings-together, a few of you have risked sharing your concerns over issues you see looming in this church's future, only to seek me out later and say: "I wouldn't want you to get the wrong idea from our conversation the other night. This really is a great church." Which it is. And I know it. But you wouldn't care whether I knew it if you weren't just a little bit anxious about the impression you might be giving ... or I might be getting.

But our mutual anxiety is not without precedent. Given a new assignment ... and more-than-adequately equipped with the tools to do it ... the disciples experienced no small amount of anxiety around the readiness issue. There they were, out in a boat ... where they fished all night and got royally skunked. Seven men with nets at the ready went o-for-the-evening. Zip. Zero. Whitewashed. Nothing. And as Roger Lovette notes: "This little story of night fishing is as old as time itself, in that the disciples used all their expertise ... all their talent ... all their know-how ... and nothing happened." Which sounds like an occasional page out of the diary of every pastor I know. In fact, it is as much every pastor's story as it is their story ... just as it is as much your story as it is their story. Notice that there are seven passengers in that boat. Five of them are named (Peter, Thomas, Nathanael, and Zebedee's boys, Jimmy and John). But who are the other two? You know as well as I do who they are. You and me. That's who they are.

All of us are in that boat. We are out there fishing. At night. All night. Which, taken at face value, is something I know precious little about. I don't fish much, even though I have a home on the water. I have caught only one fish in my life. Fortunately, that was a 13-pound King Salmon. So I retired undefeated. But, for purposes of this story, my trophy doesn't count. That's because I caught him in the daylight.

But it doesn't matter if I can't fish for fish. Because this isn't a story about fishing for fish. None of the stories in the Gospel of John are ever about what they seem to be about. They are always about something more. Which is why they are so delightful ... albeit demanding. You've got to peel them like an onion. And sometimes, when you get to the sweet stuff, it can make you cry.

Fishing, of course, is (in this story) a euphemism for "working." And not just any kind of "working," but rather the work which Jesus has prepped his disciples to do. In this story, fishing is not the disciples' way of getting away from work, but going to work. Fishing is not for bluegills and crappies. Fishing is for Jews and Gentiles ... men and women ... insiders and outsiders ... the lost, and those who are too dumb to know they are lost. To fail at fishing is not (for the purposes of this story) to fail at recreation ... but to fail at vocation. The disciples went out to "do something" for Jesus. But they couldn't. And it wasn't for lack of hard work. For in Luke's version of the same story, the disciples tell Jesus: "We toiled all night and nothing happened." What does that mean? It means that sometimes shear effort alone won't do it.

Do you know that studies of pastors who are in trouble in their churches report that those pastors work 25% harder than ordinary clergy? Hard work (however valuable) doesn't necessarily guarantee success.

Neither do the disciples come up empty because of poor timing. For in John's gospel, this fishing expedition takes place almost immediately after the resurrection. And if there was ever a time when it should have been a "piece of cake" for the followers of Jesus to climb onward and upward for Jesus, it should have been right after the resurrection. I can't think of anything more motivational. Except they couldn't sustain it. Part of the problem was that Jesus was no longer with them. "We can't do it without the Lord," they said. "Things went fine when He was here. But now He's not." And we know what that is like, don't we? Because each of us has someone in our life that we feel we can't function without. Someone dies … and we can't do it. Someone splits ... and we can't do it. Someone retires … and we can't do it. "It isn't the same," we say. Which is true. And which is sometimes immobilizing.

A little night fishing. Notice how dark it can get when you try … and you try … and you come up empty. No wonder we are a little nervous today. That's because we know what the stakes are. And we know (from reading this story) what can happen. I have reason to know it better than anybody. This is not the old familiar place anymore, and you are not the old familiar faces. This is (if you will allow me to change the sporting metaphor) a whole new ballgame. Which gives me a nice segue into my most recent version of my unpreparedness dream. It is early spring. February. I am in Lakeland, Florida. The place is Marchant Stadium ... the home of the Tigers. Sparky spots me in the stands, where I am really quite comfortable. He calls me down. "Ritter," he says, "it's time to see what you can do." So I am sent to third base. Except I have no glove. Which I tell Sparky. But Sparky doesn't care. Travis Fryman (playing next to me) doesn't care. Nobody cares. Nobody, that is, except members of the opposition, who are beginning to point at the glove-less third baseman and chortle with glee. Which is when I wake up and do not go back to sleep. And which is when I notice that I am drenched in sweat. What is the dream saying? Simply this ... that in the seventh inning of my life, I fear that I am being sent out there empty handed.

Except I'm not. And neither are you. Follow the text carefully. In the dim half-light of dawn ... silhouetted against the shoreline where fear and fatigue meet ... He meets us. And we know that it's daybreak whether the clock says so or not. For there is one kind of daybreak we experience when the sun comes up. And there is another kind of daybreak we experience when the Son breaks in.

And then I hear Him speak (as He did so long ago, to others in the same boat). And what He says is this: "Drop your nets in one more time." Which is not exactly what I expected Him to say, given that it sounds (for all the world) like, "Ritter, keep on doing what you've been doing."

And what is it that I have been doing, that I am now being called to do "one more time"? Well, the bottom line of what I do is that I tell an old, old story with as much eloquence, erudition, and passion as I can muster … trusting that if I can revive it, you can apply it, and God will approve it. In short, I preach. I do other things. But this is the thing I seemingly "have" to do. When a reporter asked Kirk Gibson why, after all the injuries, the time away, and the hassles of management, he decided to come back and give it one more shot, Gibby shrugged his shoulders and quoted Muhammed Ali who once answered a similar question with the simple declarative sentence: "A boxer boxes." The Apostle Paul would have understood that given his utterance: "Woe be unto me if I do not preach the Gospel." What Paul meant was: "Of all the things in my life over which I have some degree of choice, preaching is the one thing I can't not do." I suppose that just as "fish gotta swim and birds gotta fly," some of us gotta preach.

This has been a hard week for me. Ask my wife. She'll tell you. To be sure, I unpacked all of the boxes and arranged all of my books. But somehow I knew that until I wrote these words … and said these words … I wouldn't (in spite of all your graciousness) begin to feel at home. For comfort comes in living out one's calling. And this is what I feel called to do … morning, night … darkness, light … full, empty … companioned, abandoned. This is what "fishing" represents to me. So it is precisely in this daring and obedient act of casting into waters that

are unknown and swirling, that people like me find people like you,
and discover that we are not alone.

First United Methodist Church
Birmingham, Michigan
June 27, 1993

3

It's Got To Be Said

Scripture: Genesis 25:29-34, 27:1-19

Over the last 25 years, I keep running into people who want me to say more about the sermon that referred to my father. In a pair of congregations, it even led to multi-week adult education seminars which were co-led by my friend and pastoral colleague, Dr. Wes Brun.

Let me launch right into this with a story that is so perfect ... so fitting ... so right ... it would be a crying shame if it turned out not to be true. It concerns a young man who went off to college. Upon reaching the dormitory, he began to unpack his suitcases. Apparently, his mother had done his packing for him. In the process of putting clothing into drawers, he discovered two long, narrow pieces of cloth among the shirts, socks, and underwear. They were neatly folded and ironed. At first, he didn't know what they were. But when he looked at the design, he recognized the pattern as being one that he had seen before. At last, it came to him. These were the strings of his mother's favorite apron.

That's a powerful message. It is also a wonderful gift. It embraces everything the Bible means when it talks about "the blessing." To some of us it comes easily, graciously, and in the natural course of things. To others of us, it doesn't. Consider John Claypool … an admired colleague and a late-in-life friend … who died in the year just past, but not before he did me the honor of writing the foreword to my first book.

Once upon a time, in the springtime of his career, John Claypool was the brightest star in the constellation of the Southern Baptist denomination. A "ministerial meteor" was what some called him. As the pastor of a three thousand member church before he was thirty, he preached sermons worth hearing and wrote books worth reading. But following the death of his ten-year-old daughter from leukemia, he went through a divorce. More to the point, divorce felled him, and he was forced to reinvent himself as an Episcopalian.

But writing about his early life, long before any of this happened, he claimed to have felt less than adequate, certain that (in the eyes of those who mattered most) he amounted to very little.

"Most of all," he wrote, "I craved the approval of my mother. I longed to see a twinkle of delight in her eye and feel that she was really proud of me, something I had never felt before. There was an atmosphere of marked anxiety in my mother's attitude toward my sister and me. She seemed quite uneasy about how we were going to turn out. But being a seasoned manipulator by this time, I knew exactly what held the most promise of gaining this particular reward. My grandfather had been a minister, and the church was the only institution that mattered to my mother. So in my calculating heart of hearts, I reasoned that becoming a minister would get my mother's approval. When I made my choice of career public and wrote my parents about it,
I remember licking the envelope and saying with genuine anticipation: 'Now, at last, I will be sparkled on by my mama.'"[1]

You would be surprised how many ministers have (in their background) a strong-willed and emotionally-withholding mother. It has been suggested that a great many male clergy heed the call of their Heavenly Father as a way of working out a relationship with their earthly mother. Ironically, when John Claypool finally experienced the reality of God's grace in his own life (many years and much pain later), one of the phrases he used to describe the feeling was to say: "It suddenly dawned on me that there had been worth in me from the very beginning." Well, not everybody knows that. And not everybody feels that. Some of you don't know it now. Some of you haven't felt it ever.

Esau knew the feeling. You remember the story. Esau was the firstborn; his brother, Jacob, the second. A starving Esau returned from the field to find his brother cooking soup. Before the story was five verses old, Jacob had traded a chunk of bread and a cup of broth for Esau's birthright. Much later in the story, old Isaac (the father of the boys) was dying. He sought an audience with Esau in order that he might bestow upon his firstborn the blessing of the family. But Jacob, at the urging of his mother, conspired to dress in his brother's clothing, covered his skin with the hair of an animal, and even cultivated a scent that masqueraded as his brother's smell. Into the tent of his half-blind father went Jacob under the cover of darkness. He emerged, moments later, with the blessing that was owed to Esau.

When Esau discovered the deception, he cried with a great and bitter cry, imploring his father: "Bless me, even me also, O my father!" Yet, in the primitive Hebrew patriarchal family structure, there was but one blessing per family. And Esau had lost it. His pain was not over the loss of a theological concept but over the deeply personal words from his father which he would never hear.

Now before we push this matter further, I need to explain something to you. And that concerns the difference between birthrights and blessings. A birthright is easy to understand, in that it was usually economic in nature. Who gets the money when dad dies? Who gets the farm? The fields? The sheep and the oxen? All the stuff in the barn? The gold watch he got from his daddy? That kind of thing.

That's birthright business.

Blessings, however, were more personal ... and covered a wider range of promises. The blessing was that gift of a dying father by which the powers that enhanced life (such as peace, prosperity, fertility, wisdom, and victory in battle) were allegedly passed from one generation to another. More than money, houses, and land, the blessing sought to pass the benefits of the good life. It was a way of saying: "Look, these are the fruits of life that I have worked hard to achieve. These are the gifts and the graces, the virtues and the lessons, that I have taken a lifetime to learn. Take them and run with them. They are yours now."

Over time, however, the blessing was broadened to include all children, and became equated with what might be called "a rite of passage." It was a way of saying: "May God go with you and look after you. My own hopes and best wishes go with you. You have my permission to get on with your life. Go with my blessing. Be who you are. Become who you will become. I am still vitally interested in everything you attempt. I may not understand everything you are. I may not approve of everything you do. I will still watch over you with a mixture of anxiety and expectation. But take my words as permission to get on with whatever life has in store for you....or whatever you have in store for life."

Friends, that's important stuff. That's what people tell me every time I raise this "blessing business." In fact, people share the most amazing stories about getting the blessing or about not getting it. All of which tells me two things. First, this matter of the blessing can weigh pretty heavily upon you, until you get it resolved. And second, it is extremely hard to give something to your children if you have never received it from your parents.

Earlier, in my story about apron strings, I gave you an example of an unspoken blessing ... a gift of cloth, packed away in a suitcase. But in the limited time I have left, I would like to make a case for words rather than gestures ... suggesting that (where blessings are concerned) there is incredible power in the spoken word. When we were children, we used to stick our thumbs in our ears, wiggle our fingers, and return the taunts of our enemies by saying: "Sticks and stones may break my bones, but words will never hurt me." How wrong we were. And how little we knew it at the time. Words do hurt. Words also heal. Words have incredible power to build us up or tear us down. Apparently, the author of Proverbs 18:21 thought so too, for he wrote: "Death and life are in the power of the tongue."

Feeling backed into a corner in a marriage counseling session, a man whose twenty-year marriage was coming unglued lashed out: "I told my wife I loved her on our wedding day and it stands until I revoke it." Another, in response to his wife's plaintive question, "Do you love me, John?" responded: "I'm here, ain't I?" Well, I suppose there's something to that. But not enough.

My father, who departed this earth just two months after my firstborn son entered it, was a very intelligent man. It did not take a genius to realize that he may have been a genius. But he lacked the credentials to prove it. He dropped out of Northwestern High School one semester before graduating. He never went back. He never went on. It handicapped him all his life. My father never worked one day in a job that taxed even a quarter of the ability he possessed.

When I went to college and seminary, I think he felt proud. I also think he felt mocked, envious, and more than a little embarrassed. My academic success at Albion and Yale was a visual display of a future he could have had but chose not to. The further I went in higher education, the worse it made him feel about himself. He never said so (at least not in so many words). In fact, he never said much of anything about my schooling, which was one of the ways I could tell it bothered him. After correcting my ignorance, he would say: "Well, I guess you don't know everything." Or he would compliment himself with a put-down by saying: "I guess your old man isn't as dumb as some people seem to think he is."

It hurt to hear him say things like that. It hurt to not hear him say other, more positive things about my progress. It hurt, even more, when he didn't feel up to making the trip to New Haven in June of 1965. The occasion was my graduation from Yale. He sent my mother and sister. He stayed in Detroit.

Very early on a Saturday morning, in August of 1967, the phone rang in my parsonage in Dearborn. Half awake, I answered it. It was my mother saying that she thought my father was dead. She was right. He was. I told her to make the necessary calls. I told her I would be right over. I got there after the police and before the coroner. Not knowing what to do at a time like that, and not really wanting to talk to anybody or sit and look at his body, I thought I would go through his papers. I figured that I might find something that the coroner or the funeral director might need. I didn't have the faintest idea what I was looking for. I didn't even have the faintest idea why I was looking.

But I started with his wallet and struck a strange kind of pay dirt. There, tucked away behind a few dollar bills, I found several worn sheets of copy paper. They were tissue thin and deeply creased by much folding and unfolding. I removed them, opened them, and quickly realized that I didn't need to read them. For I had seen them before. They were copies of my grades from all four years at Albion and all three years at Yale. I knew why he'd kept them. I found myself wondering how many times he'd pulled them out and shown them to somebody, speaking of his son, the student, with pride. I only wish that he'd been able to tell me.

•••••••

And Isaac said to his son: "Come near. Kiss me. Your smell is that of a field which the Lord has smiled upon. May he give you the dew of heaven. May he give you the fatness of earth. May he give you plenty of grain … plenty of wine. May peoples serve you. May nations bow down to you. Cursed be those who curse you. Blessed be those who bless you."

And God, who was not nearly so poetic in speaking to His son as Isaac was in speaking to his, came no less powerfully to the point when He was overheard saying to Jesus: "You are my beloved son. I am pleased with you."

Well, whether it was the voice of your mother's apron strings in the suitcase, God's voice in the cloud, or something far more ordinary but no less beautiful, I hope the words once came to you. But I am not overly concerned this morning with the words that came to you. My primary concern is with the words that need to come through you. For there are people near you, who may very much need to hear them.

Ted Turner is a household name in the state of Georgia. He is equally well known across the nation. He is, by everybody's definition, a high achiever. He is a multi-millionaire, a businessman extraordinaire, a cable television entrepreneur, and the owner of numerous other enterprises, including the Atlanta Braves. He has also made his mark in the world of yacht racing, achieving an international reputation as a sportsman. For gosh sakes, the man was once even married to Jane Fonda. One wonders if there are any mountains left for Turner to climb. But he tells an interesting story about himself. Riding the crest of his numerous triumphs, he went out alone in his boat one day, journeying well beyond the sight of land. He dropped anchor, cut the engine and sat quietly for a while. He was trying to sort out what was happening in his life (factoring the rewards earned against the energies required to earn them). He wondered what he had been trying to prove. He also wondered who he had been trying to prove it to. At last, he stood on the deck, looked out at some far distant point where the sea and sky meet, and cried out to his father: "Is this good enough?"

My friends, there are people close to you … some of them sharing a home with you … who may very well be wondering the same thing and waiting for an answer.

Northville United Methodist Church
Northville, Michigan
July 2007

4

Confessions of a Reluctant Hugger

Scripture: Mark 5:21-34

The seeds of this sermon were first planted at Newburg U. M C. in Livonia, MI in the 1970's. They finally bloomed into a sermon in the 1980's at Nardin Park and then were transplanted multiple times including this 1996 incarnation in Birmingham.

I once heard someone say that there are only two kinds of people in the world ... those who insist on dividing the world into two kinds of people, and those who don't. But for those who enjoy such divisions, one that I would have you consider this morning is between those who hug (especially those who hug powerfully and repeatedly) and those who don't.

I will confess to being a non-hugger ... or (at least) to having been a non-hugger. I am getting better at it. But it has not always been easy or natural. Let me hasten to add that I never had much trouble hugging if the mood was right, the place was right, and the huggee was right. But when the issue became something other than passion, I was never one of those instant embracers, able to squeeze and clutch on cue. I do not come from a generation of huggers, or a family of huggers. We cared about each other. And we were able to show that we cared about each other. But our depiction of affection was always quiet, reserved, and mildly understated.

In the early days of my ministry (during the mid-to-late 60's), sensitivity training was all the rage. For days at a time ... and sometimes for hours on end ... we explored what it was like to get "in touch" with our feelings. We wrestled with such questions as to how we were perceived in a group ... how we related to a group ... and how we could learn to trust and be trusted in a group. I remember one particular exercise where we were blindfolded, placed in a circle, and encouraged to let our body go limp. Then the encircling group would push us every which way, even as they supported us, lest we fall. It was physical. It was emotional. It felt good when I tried it. But I would hardly call it a breakthrough experience.

Then in 1980, when I was preparing to leave my congregation in Livonia for a new congregation in Farmington Hills, I felt limited by my accustomed means of saying thank you and farewell. With many of those people, a good word and a firm handshake simply wouldn't suffice. I needed to give something more. So hugs became the order of the hour. I gave myself permission to give them … get them … and enjoy them. And, with them, I turned a corner in my life. Not abruptly. Not dramatically. But at a pace that allowed me to remain who I was, even as I began to explore who I was becoming. I still envy the truly expansive huggers of the world … and perhaps mildly fear them. But ever so slowly, I am becoming more like them … to my greater benefit, I think … and to my greater pleasure.

For none of us is totally free from what psychologist Sidney Simon once called "skin hunger." We need the physical closeness of other human beings. We crave it. We can't live without it. There are all kinds of studies about the role of human touch in the nurturing of an infant. If a kid doesn't get held … doesn't get cradled … doesn't get rocked and carried … the kid doesn't develop. It's that simple. Which is why some of the most technologically sophisticated neo-natal units now come equipped with "designated rockers." These are people who don't do anything medically or pharmacologically. All they do is rock babies. Skin hunger. We start with a lot of it. And a case can be made that we never really outgrow it.

But, in many of us, there's an equally powerful and competitive need known as "space hunger." We need room. Some of us need more room than others. I have a pair of esteemed colleagues in the ministry who are both friends of mine, but neither is particularly fond of the other. That's because one of them regularly (and repeatedly) crowds the other's space. He can't talk to you without putting his arm on you ... or around you. If you back off, he moves in. If some part of his body isn't making physical contact with some part of yours, he feels uncomfortably distant. But when he gets where he needs to be in order to feel comfortable, my other friend feels invaded. It's not something that is easy to explain. But it is something that is easy to understand.

All of us have different needs. And all of us have different comfort zones. Were I to stop the sermon right now and encourage you to get up and greet your neighbor, some of you would do so enthusiastically, while some would do so reluctantly. But you would all do it. However, if I told you to embrace your neighbor ... exchange signs of brotherly and sisterly affection with your neighbor ... or bestow upon your neighbor a holy kiss (all of which would carry the weight of the New Testament injunction) ... I would divide (and perhaps empty) the house. I'll never forget my colleague's report of the woman who angrily exited his church just after he announced his instructions for the congregation's observance of the "Ritual of Friendship." When the head usher finally caught up to this lady in the parking lot (and inquired as to whether any particular emergency had occasioned her exit), she barked at him without ever breaking stride: "Just go back and tell your preacher that I didn't come to church to be touched by strangers."

Some people recoil from touch because they have been hurt in the past and are afraid of being hurt in the future. Somebody got too close and presumed upon that closeness ... violating them physically, sexually, or emotionally. Last Friday afternoon, during a staff retreat at First Baptist Church, I picked up one of Steve Jones's sermons during the break. Steve is a good guy, and I enjoy reading his stuff. Later that night, I read Steve's account of the woman who, when she first came into his church, never looked anyone in the eye. Instead, she looked at the floor ... almost always with a sad expression. On the rare occasion when she smiled, her smile was always forced and fleeting. And Steve had the good sense not to touch her. For she sent signals that it would never be acceptable to hug her or take her hand. Over time, he learned that the only way she could comfortably converse with him was if he placed his hands behind his back. That way she could neither see them nor feel any threat from them. And her name (as the Bible says) is "legion."

Other people recoil from touch because they have been conditioned to acquaint physicality with sexuality. I am in possession of a document (given to me at a clergy seminar where the attendance of every United Methodist pastor was mandatory) entitled "Is This Touch Necessary?" It calls upon clergy to reconsider everything we do with our hands and arms, lest we send signals that might be misconstrued or wrongly responded to. There is, within the document, an extended discourse on hugging. How many seconds are too many seconds? How much body is too much body? The questions are pointed. And the warnings are even more specific. Never hug anyone in private. If absolutely necessary, always hug people in public. Never in the office. Never at night. Perhaps in the narthex ... after the 11:00 service ... on a Sunday ... if at all. And after reading paragraphs upon paragraphs of cautions and conditions, the bottom line was somewhere between "when in doubt, don't" and "if you keep your arms at your side, you'll never be sorry."

And then there is the related problem of men hugging other men. After all, how might that be misconstrued? Which probably explains why men, when they hug each other, feel the need to pound on each other's back with fists or open hands. It looks athletic. And anything that looks athletic could hardly be misconstrued as something affectionate.

Still, others recoil from touch out of fear that too much will be revealed, should someone get too close. One of the soft-rock ballads of the 70s that can still be heard on the easy-listening stations of Detroit is the Dan Hill tune which contains this refrain:

> *Sometimes when we touch, the honesty's too much,*
> *And I have to close my eyes and hide.*
> *I want to hold you till I die,*
> *Till we both break down and cry.*
> *I want to hold you till the fear in me subsides.*

Where does the fear come from? Damned if I know. But it's there.

And acts of affection will reveal it … before they heal it. The nearer people get, the more vulnerable they become. Which is one very good reason why kids should avoid become overly involved, sexually. Not because they are incapable of handling the mechanics involved, but because they are so ill equipped to handle the emotions involved. They tell me, "Don't worry, we've taken care of things." But the real issue … the deeper issue … the profoundly personal issue … is not whether they can take care of "things," but whether they can take care of each other. Intimacy is not so much about getting at someone's skin, as getting inside someone's skin … or under someone's skin … in ways that are never easy to understand or respond to. It is far from accidental that husbands and wives often pick an argument with each other within hours of the sharing of wonderful intimacy with each other. Why? Because they are uncomfortable being so close and will work (subconsciously or otherwise) to reestablish some distance between them. What does the song say: "Sometimes when we touch, the honesty's too much"?

And yet … in spite of all our caution and reticence … we know that there is an important issue here. We know that in order to be "in touch," we must (to some degree) be in touch. Literally. Let me try to explain it by telling you how I stumbled upon it pastorally, before confirming it biblically.

About fifteen or twenty years ago, I began to touch people when I prayed for them in the hospital. I didn't think it through before I began to do it. I just started doing it. Usually, I take their hand when I pray for them. But if they are in a coma (or if their hand is unavailable to me because of a variety of needles, tubes, restraints, etc.) I touch their forehead or their shoulder. Nobody has ever withdrawn a hand. Virtually everyone extends one. It's funny I never noticed that in the early days of ministry.

And there is something powerful that happens during that period of praying and handholding. Don't ask me what it is. But I can feel it. I can feel the fear (hitherto unacknowledged). Moreover, if my prayer is asking for this individual to be held through the pain … held through the night … held through the surgery … or held through the valley … is it really fair for me to ask of God, something that I am not willing to ask of myself? Further still, nearly every touch a patient receives in the hospital is unpleasantly invasive. They are probed. They are poked. Things are inserted. Their daily routine includes innumerable needles, thermometers, and catheters. Except for a morning sponge bath, my hand may be the only touch that is non-invasively redemptive.

Then, one day, it occurred to me that every major pastoral transition point is also a "handsy" kind of thing. I baptize a baby … with hands. I confirm a teenager … with hands. I consecrate a marriage … with hands. And on the few occasions when I have had the privilege of helping ordain a ministerial candidate into the lifelong service of Jesus Christ, how is it done? You guessed it. With hands.

And then there's this unfinished biblical business from our texts this morning. Two stories. Healing stories. Both involving touch. Sort of.

In the first story, a ruler of the synagogue (Jairus, by name) comes to Jesus in a panic. He tells Jesus that his little girl is at the point of death. Then follows the request: "Come, lay your hands on her, that she may be well." And when Jesus is rushing off to do just that, he crosses paths with a widow. She is suffering from a twelve-year flow of blood. She elbows her way through the crowd surrounding Jesus, saying: "If I touch the hem of his garment, I shall be healed."

It is the second story that interests me the most, given that it interrupts the first. Which is how much of my pastoral work presents itself to me ... as an interruption of something else I was doing or planning to do.

The woman is distraught ... but expectant. Distraught, because her flow of blood has lasted a dozen years. Distraught, because she has gone through all of the doctors in the Yellow Pages, along with all of her money. Distraught, because she is no better, only worse. Distraught, because feminine blood flow has rendered her sexually, sociologically and spiritually unclean. Which means that she can't do anything in the presence of anybody. And should others touch her ... or be touched by her ... they will be rendered as unclean as she. Still, however, she is expectant ... even to the point of saying: "This is the day it all comes to a halt ... my bleeding from the inside ... my banishment from the outside."

And when Jesus spins towards his disciples and shouts: "Who touched me?" it is not because he is irritated, but because he genuinely wants to know. Even though he is on his way to a deathbed, he doesn't want to let this healing moment slip by unnoticed. One can hear him saying: "I think I just helped somebody, and I want to know who." Again, I can identify.

Don't underestimate what we have here. What we have are a pair of hands-on-healings, enacted by a hands-on Lord. Sure, it's not the only way to be healed. Jesus even healed one disease long distance, sending the summoning messenger back home on a twenty-four-hour journey ... but not before saying: "By the time you get home, the matter you inquired about will have been taken care of." Which it was. But, more often than not, touching and curing seemed to go (if you will pardon the expression) hand-in-hand. Moments ago we sang (with obvious relish and feeling):

> *He touched me O he touched me,*
> *And O the joy that floods my soul!*
> *Something happened, and now I know,*
> *He touched me and made me whole.*

And I am sure that some of you said, "Ah, that's lovely. But it's only a figure of speech, you know. Because Jesus can't really touch anybody ... anymore ... save in some spiritual way."

But, my friends, maybe that's why we're here ... to do in a physical way what Jesus can only do in a spiritual way. So may God find ways to bless the huggers of the kingdom, even as God quietly damns the church that sits on its hands.

First United Methodist Church
Birmingham, Michigan
June 30, 1996

5

Could I Have This Dance for the Rest of My Life?

Scripture: Genesis 29:1-20

Over the years I have heard (and read) hundreds of sermons on the subject of love. Never have I heard a sermon on the subject of romance. So, I finally wrote one. This version was preached while doing an interim at New Hope U.M.C.in Shelby Twp., MI.

There was a certain woman whose young daughter was very ill. The mother went to the pharmacy to secure a prescription for her daughter. As she returned to her car, she realized she had locked her keys inside. She remembered having heard that a coat hanger could be used to open a locked car door. So she began to look around. Sure enough, in a nearby flowerbed, she found one. But what to do with it.

In desperation, she bowed her head and asked God to send help. Within five minutes, a dirty, scruffy man pulled up on a beat-up old motorcycle. The woman thought: "So this is what God has sent me." Nevertheless, she breathed a prayer of thanks and told him her story. "My daughter is very sick. I stopped to get some medicine but locked my keys in the car. Can you use this coat hanger to help me?" "Sure," he grumbled. In a flash, he had the door open. She responded, "Thank you so much. You are a very nice man." He responded, "Lady, I am no nice man. I'm an ex-con. I was in prison for car theft." Whereupon the woman lunged at him with a hug and cried out, "Thank you, God, you even sent me a professional."

Well, I did not ride up on a motorcycle. And having showered and shaved this very morning, I hope I do not strike you as "dirty and scruffy." And if you locked your keys in your car, I am no good with a coat hanger (although if a brick is handy, I will be glad to throw it through your window). But I have framed certificates on my wall that say that I am a professional. I can do this. I told your pastor I would do this. And now I stand before you ready to do this.

Preach, I mean. But what to preach? I could talk about the season of Lent which is very much upon us. Or I could draw one last sermon out of the season of Epiphany, which is a week or so behind us. I could consult the Lectionary, but your pastor told me that such was not his customary practice. And then there was the Super Bowl, but I am not sure I can draw anything meaty from that. So I decided to begin my thought processes with Valentine's Day. I mean, how many sermons have you ever heard on the subject of romance. All I know is that you are about to hear one now. And to those who want me to get personal, yes I remembered the card. The flowers. Dinner at a top-drawer restaurant. I'm on it. The whole nine yards.

I recall the TV news story about the harried father, three small kids in tow, racing through the mall at 8:30 pm on February 13th. When asked by the interviewer if he was doing a little last minute shopping, he confessed that he was headed to Victoria's Secret where he planned to spend $300 on his wife. I found myself wondering how he was going to explain his purchases to his kids. I am sure one of them would ask him, "What's mommy going to do with those things, daddy?" Or he could have spent $19.95 and bought the book, "Why Men Don't Have A Clue, and Women Always Need More Shoes."

I've spent a lot of time around people who are romantic, having officiated (by actual count) over 1,600 weddings. But while the ceremony is by far and away the most dramatic moment of a wedding, the initial conversation I have with the bride and groom is the most revealing one. The best way for a pastor to spark conversation among those about to be married is to ask them where they met ... how they met ... how long ago they met ... whether they felt anything (or even liked each other) when they met ... and how they got from meeting to dating, and from dating to committing. Such questions are icebreakers, given that while very few couples want to talk to preachers, almost all couples love to talk about themselves.

But things have changed over the years. Today's couples coming to the altar are considerably older than they used to be. Moreover, they have been "an item" considerably longer than they used to be. Which should bode well for marital stability in the future, although the numbers aren't saying so yet. Or, to boil it down to something you can remember, the majority of my brides have reached the age of twenty-eight, the length of most courtships is four years, and the majority of those about to be wed were either introduced by friends or began as friends. Truth be told, many had been friends for a considerable amount of time before one of them made a move that turned the friendship into something romantic.

Still, a few people tell of love at first sight. Two or three times a year, someone will say, "We met, and later that night I told my best friend that I had just met the person I was going to marry." I always like those stories, given that I was "hooked" in the fourth or fifth hour of our eleven-hour first date. That date took place on a Sunday, mind you. And it started with church, mind you. But, hey, I move fast. Jacob would have understood, given that he fell both early and hard for Rachel. It happened when Jacob was on the run from his brother, Esau, who might have murdered Jacob, had he caught up with him. But that's another story for another day. This is our story for this day. And it may be one of the most lovely (and quite possible the only) boy-meets-girl story in Holy Scripture.

Like I said, Jacob is on the run (heading east) when he comes upon a well with a few sheep and some shepherds hanging out around it. While all of them are thirsting, nobody's drinking. Because the well is covered, don't you see … covered by a capstone that is so big and heavy that it takes a bevy of men to lift it. Now it is possible that the capstone was large and heavy on purpose. Because, if it wasn't, then one man could lift it. And if one man could lift it, a solitary shepherd (arriving alone) might take more than his fair share of precious water. So the tradition developed that nobody would uncap the well until all of the "locals" were at the well. Which is why Jacob is at the well when Rachel approaches with her father's sheep.

Now Jacob doesn't know Rachel. But he knows he has relatives back east, and he is told by loitering shepherds that Rachel is connected to his relatives. As to exactly how we can't be sure. But none of that matters at the moment. What matters is that when Jacob and Rachel see each other, sparks fly between them. Cue the violins if you please.

Now, remember that the stone requires several men to move it. Well, Jacob rolls it away single-handedly. Whereupon he waters Rachel's flocks, kisses Rachel's lips and breaks into tears. After which he waits seven years, followed by an additional seven years, to marry her … working all that time for her father. And the Bible says, "Those years seemed to him as but a few days, so great was his love for her." More violins, please … and maybe a sprinkling of Sinatra.

Jacob and Rachel met at a well … kissed at a well … and fell in love at a well. You might as well call it a watering hole. And although everybody claims to hate such places (watering holes, I mean), you'd be surprised how many of my brides and grooms actually met at one. I'm glad that Kris and I met in church. Because if we had met at a bar, I'd probably have to make up a story.

As concerns the meeting of lovers, is it fate? Who knows? But when it works, it feels that way. Or is it God? Again, when it works, it feels that way. When two people tell me, "they were meant to be together," I figure they are talking the language of ecstasy more than the language of theology. They are saying:

> What we found … what we feel … indeed, what we have is so deep, so moving, so profound, so life-changing, that it must have had its origin in a Mind greater than ours. I mean, we weren't even looking for anybody at that point in our lives.

Fifty years ago, we sat around a campfire and sang:

> *Tell me why the stars do shine*
> *Tell me why the ivy twines*
> *Tell me why the sky's so blue*
> *And I will tell you just why I love you.*

> *I really think that God above*

Created you for me to love
He picked you out from all the rest
Because God knew I'd love you best.

But I don't think we were singing about how God was working so much as how we were feeling ... believing that nothing could feel this good if it did not come from God, and no one could feel this good if he (she) did not come from God. And while I am too much of a Wesleyan to believe in predestination, I'll gladly concede that, in some cases, heaven may have something to do with fluttering hearts and all that follows. Although a fifty percent divorce rate confounds such a philosophy, leading many to ask, "Does God mislead, or do we misread?" I frankly don't know whether some marriages might be made in heaven. What I do know is that in every marriage, some assembly is required.

Which is why many of us try to hedge our bets with science ... most recently computer science. Not long ago, I talked to a fellow who met his fiancé on EHarmony.com. You know how it goes. You answer a slew of questions. You list your likes and dislikes, followed by your desires and needs. You identify the top five things that attract you. Then you add the top five things that repulse you. A profile is created. Then your profile becomes part of a network. Truth be told, I am quite impressed by how sophisticated this process has become.

So I asked this fellow to describe his experience. Once his data was made available to the general public, he got eighty hits on his profile. From the eighty hits, he got twenty-two Internet conversations with females. From the twenty-two conversations, he got ten first dates. From the ten first dates, he got one second date. But the second date failed to lead to a third date. So he decided to redo his profile. Starting from scratch, he was more successful in the second round. He met Wanda Wonderful, and they were married. I did it. Or EHarmony did it. Or maybe God did it. You tell me. Unfortunately, they are now divorced.

For the truth is, no matter how perfect the methodology, it can't guarantee chemistry. "I don't know why I love you like I do. I don't know why I just do." Which sounded stupid when someone sang it sixty years go. But we haven't gotten that far beyond it. Or, as Ezio Pinza (in the musical South Pacific) sang after meeting Mary Martin:

> *Who can explain it? Who can tell us why?*
> *Fools give us reasons, wise men seldom try.*

Still, when it comes to meeting and mating, street wisdom has its place.

> Do opposites attract?
> Sure.
> But should you also have something in common?
> Sure.

Should you check out someone's family?

Sure, you're marrying the whole nine yards.

Will the same sterling personality trait that makes someone special, occasionally drive you crazy?

Sure.

Therefore, is being the right person more important than finding the right person?

Sure.

But if there is one thing that has become clear to me across the years, it is this. Most mature people can, over time, negotiate differences in their interests. But very few can negotiate differences in their core values. So pay attention to someone's core values.

I often ask couples to tell me what drew the two of them to each other. And when they say they both love to ski, they both love to watch "Big Bang Theory," they both love the color purple, and they both hate broccoli with equal intensity, I have to put my hand over my mouth to keep from saying, "big hairy deal."

I suppose it is nice when lovers share more likes than dislikes. Common activities do bond. But I have also seen ...

• Morning people work it out with night people.

• Tent campers work it out with partners who won't stay any place where they don't put a mint on your pillow.

• Life of the party types work it out with people who would rather play chess quietly in the corner.

• And, if my own marriage is any indication, I have learned that ESPN people can co-exist, even thrive, with HGTV people.

But, at the end of the day ...

• If your core value is generosity, you are going to have a hard time living with a tightwad.

• If your core value is fidelity, you are going to have a hard time living with a flirt.

• If your core value is family, you are going to have a hard time living with someone who puts anything and everything ahead of family.

• If your core value involves a belief in the basic goodness and trustworthiness of humanity, you're going to have a hard time living with someone who believes that people are out to screw you every chance they get.

• And if your core value involves religious faith, you are going to have a hard time living with someone who pays it mere lip service or, worse yet, mocks it at every turn. "You know, kids, we could go to the cottage every weekend if mommy hadn't told those ladies at the church that she would teach Sunday School."

The comforting fact that you both like Sixty Minutes, soft shell crab, and scuba diving may be great reasons for a second date. But in a marriage, most of us would rather have someone who honors our core commitments over someone who shares our favorite activities. Relationships are most likely to survive (even thrive) when the people in them give similar answers to the question, "so how do you define the good life?" And by, "the good life," I mean both, "the sweet life" and "the moral life."

One of the nice things about my job is that I see people at every stage of love's journey. Not long ago, I watched a couple put two hands on one knife and cut into a beautifully frosted cake that had the number "50" etched in the icing. Children there. Grandchildren there. Old and dear friends there. Candles on the tables. Carnations in the vases. Gifts in the corner. Videos on the screen. Laughter at the video, but tears too, when faces appeared on the screen who were no longer on the scene.

Then the groom of fifty years ... an intensely private man who hates speaking in public ... banged on his glass, looked at those present, thanked them for being there, and said simply, "This is the best day of my life. There is no place I would rather be than here. And no people I would rather be with than the woman beside me and our friends and family together in this room."

•••••••

I hope Kris and I get to fifty. And, God willing, I'd like to push our finish line a whole lot further out than that.

Kristine & Bill Ritter, July 2, 1966

Stephen Covey (author of the book, "Seven Habits of Highly Effective People" reminds us to, "Always begin with the end in mind." I don't really know what end I had in mind when I started going out with Tina Larson of Novi. Well, that's not quite true. I do know what end I had in mind, but I am not about to tell you.

But I now have a different end in mind. A better end in mind. It first came into view several years ago when we were at a dance. Yes, I dance. The slow ones better than the fast ones. Along with an occasional polka, as long as there is an open floor and a supply of available oxygen.

On that evening, they had one of those reflector balls that rotate at the ceiling level, sending dancing squares of light down on the couples and making it seem as if the whole room is in motion. At that moment, there were only three or four couples left out there. All of us had some age on us. So the DJ said, "let's spin one more for the geezer set." It was a slow song, one with a three-count rhythm. It took me a few moments to adjust and then I got it. He was playing a waltz. One-two-together, two-two-together, three-two-together. And once we were able to feel it with our feet, we could hear it with our ears. It was Anne Murray, that Canadian contralto, crooning a little bit of "country." At which point it was hard to resist singing along.

> *Could I have this dance for the rest of my life?*
> *Would you be my partner every night?*
> *When we're together, it feels so right,*
> *Could I have this dance for the rest of my life?*

New Hope United Methodist Church
Shelby Twp., Michigan
February 17, 2013

Let the record show that Kris and I celebrated
our 51st Anniversary on July 2, 2017.

6

Tied to Be Fit

Scripture: Genesis 2:18-24; Ecclesiastes 4:9-12

This sermon was first preached at First U.M.C. Birmingham and later appeared as part of the book entitled "Reflections on Marriage and Spiritual Growth," edited by Andrew Weaver and Carolyn Stapleton.

The first time I met Will Willimon was during Parents Weekend at Duke University, 1993. He was reflecting on his ten years as Dean of the Chapel—which led him to the subject of weddings. Prior to his arrival at Duke, he had warned his wife that there was no way they could expect to take a summer vacation, given that he would be busy every weekend with brides and grooms. The way he figured it, kids would graduate in the spring and marry in the summer. And given the beauty of the building, at least some of them would marry at Duke Chapel.

He was dead wrong, of course. That first summer, he performed three student weddings. He could have vacationed every weekend. Today, while Duke Chapel hosts 125 weddings a year, only a few of them involve Duke Students or recent graduates. The chaplain, you see, was locked into the memory of another era—the era when I married my wife, and he married his.

Over the last 36 years, I have performed 1600 weddings, which has given me one of the better seats from which to observe the ever-changing nuptial parade. Brides and grooms are older now. Wiser, I cannot necessarily say, but definitely older. When I started out, most of them were 22 years of age and younger. The average length of courtship was two years, maybe three. They were starting out young. They were starting out poor. But everybody they knew was in the same boat. And if it bothered them, they did not show it.

Today, the average age of my brides is 28. The grooms are slightly older. The average courtship period is between five and six years. Seventy percent of my couples are living together at the time of the wedding, or have lived together previously. The last teenager I married was ten years ago. All of which interests me. But of more immediate concern is how the "changing scene" has altered my homilies (those short little sermonettes we preachers feel compelled to deliver at weddings, the better to feel that we are honoring our call and earning our honorarium). Once upon a time, my homiletical sentiments were stern and sober. I reminded everybody that marriage is a serious business and that building a life together requires hard work and discipline. I warned them that marriage will ask more of them than has ever been asked before while requiring them to go further than they have ever gone before. I told them it was not going to be a bed of roses ... moonlight and roses, wine and roses, or beer and pretzels, for that matter. I hammered hard on the anvil of old-fashioned words like "forgiveness," "persistence," and "commitment." In short, I used the six or seven minutes available to me to take the stars out of their eyes and rivet their feet to the ground. And then, with homily complete, I would announce a hymn (presumably something like "Be Strong, We Are Not Here to Play").

Now I am changing my tune. That's because so many brides and grooms are coming to the altar not only knowing that but also worrying about that. They expect marriage to be difficult and fear that it may be impossible. So I find myself looking for ways to say: "Hey, in the name of Jesus Christ, go for it. You can do it. Sure, it's gonna be hard. But it's also gonna be good. The outcome will be worth the effort. Marriage is a great thing. It's a wonderful step you're taking. We couldn't be happier for you."

This is the reason I resonated to a wedding homily I heard a colleague deliver on the biblical image of the three-strand cord (Ecclesiastics 4:9-12). So I found the text, went to work on the text, wrestled mightily with the text, fell just a little in love with the text, before tossing the words of the text in the air so that they came down and organized themselves under the title "Tied to Be Fit." For that's what the text says. It says that two will be better than one; three, better than two; and multiple-braided cords, stronger than cords of a single braid. It promises that a certain "fitness" will follow when one becomes two ... singular becomes plural ... and soloists decide to become halves of a duet (or thirds of a trio).

Ponder the text, beginning with the blunt assertion that "two are better than one" and concluding with the oft-quoted aphorism, "A threefold cord is not quickly broken."

Where do we read it? In the book of Ecclesiastes, that's where we read it. And when can we date it? Relatively late in Old Testament history (about 300 B.C.), that's when we can date it. And who wrote it? Darned if anyone knows. All we know is that King Solomon did not write it, even though the first few words of the first chapter of Ecclesiastes suggest that he did. Trust me, he did not.

As I have often suggested to skeptical congregations, the book of Ecclesiastes is a strange collection of stuff ... always realistic, seldom optimistic, occasionally pessimistic (and, for those chemically or temperamentally tilted toward the blues) more than a little depressing. Yet I, for one, like its emphasis on extracting life's sweetness wherever one happens to find it. Ecclesiastes never ventures very far from the idea that life is a tough proposition. But the author says it is even tougher for those who go it alone. This leads to the statement that "two are better than one," which sounds nice when read at a wedding. But it was not written for a wedding. And there is no evidence that the author had marriage in mind when putting pen to parchment. So who are the "two" referenced in this writing?

Scholars speculate. I have read several. Few agree. The "two" could be two friends, two siblings, two co-workers, two citizens, or two of anything. The language is pretty generic. The author is talking about the advantages of pairing up, teaming up, matching up. But since the language does not exclude marriage … and since there is a reference to keeping warm by lying down together … I am going to "hunch" that marriage is at least in the back of the author's mind, the better to move it to the front of mine.

"Two are better than one." I'll buy that even though I face a danger in saying that. For I carry out my ministry amidst a whole lot of "ones" … some of whom have never been "twos," some of whom would give their eyeteeth to be "twos," and some of whom have no interest whatsoever in becoming "twos." And then there are the "twos" who secretly harbor a desire to be "ones," figuring that "twos" is not nearly what it is cracked up to be if it means being "two with you." If any of that describes you, let me tell you that I hear you, believe you, feel with you, and will, to the degree it is pastorally possible, be there for you. I am very much aware that "one is a whole number." And I believe that the sanctuary ought to be one of those places where it is perfectly acceptable to say to the head usher upon entering, "Pew for one, please."

But I have this text to deal with, including my belief that there is truth to be gleaned from it … assuming I am clever enough to find it, bold enough to say it, and you are open enough to hear it. "Two are better than one," the author says. "Why?" you ask. "Four reasons," is the answer.

First, "two are better than one" because they have a good return for their work. I suspect that this reflected an agricultural era when one extra body meant two extra hands, therefore doubling the amount that could be planted, picked, served, or sold. I remember what people used to say about employing junior high boys; one boy is one boy, two boys are half a boy, and three boys are no boy at all. But this is not generally true of adults. Two adults tend to work harder and produce more. One of the delightful things we are learning in today's marital culture is that it does not really matter who does what work … only that shared work feels better and yields more.

Here, let me take a moment to talk about work that is done alongside my work (intimately adjacent to my work). Twenty-five years ago, it became increasingly fashionable for persons married to clergy to differentiate themselves from the work of clergy. "We are clergy spouses," they said. "We are not clergy assistants. Therefore, do not expect us to play the pianos nobody else wants to play, run the programs nobody else wants to run, teach the classes nobody else wants to teach, or sweep the corners nobody else wants to sweep. Congregations are not paying for two. Therefore, congregations have no right to require (or expect) the work of two."

As a speech, it was long overdue and much needed. But speaking for myself, I cannot tell you what a blessing it has been to be married to someone who believes that churches are good places to be, that church people are good people to be with, that the ministry is a calling that spills over and embraces both sides of a marriage, and that there are tasks within the ministry that suit her gifts and that she can and does do (willingly, graciously, and more productively than anybody has reason to require or expect). Her own career notwithstanding, our "two" has been far better than my "one." And my congregations have received incredible returns from our mutuality of effort.

But there are other kinds of returns for the "good work of two" ... returns not necessarily measurable in field or marketplace. I am talking about returns related to the raising of children and preparing them for marriages of their own.

We know ... and the documentation gets stronger by the day ... that intact marriages will produce children who get higher grades, are arrested less often, and remain freer from addictions and pregnancies than kids from marriages that split (or marriages that never occurred in the first place). To be sure, there are exceptions to every rule. And there are some incredible parenting jobs being done solo (or across the divorce divide). But everything I see and read tells me that there are measurable payoffs for kids who grow up in marriages that remain stable. And those payoffs continue in succeeding generations. The single measurable factor that will increase the likelihood that your children will make long-lasting marriages of their own is not their age, their job, their wealth, or their level of education prior to marrying, but whether they come to matrimony with their birth parents still married to each other.

Talking with a woman whose primary complaint about her husband was "there's just nothing there … he no longer makes me happy," I asked about the impact a divorce might have on her minor children. Leading her to ask, "Are you suggesting I should stay in an unhappy marriage just for the sake of my kids?" To which I replied, "I can't answer for you. But knowing what I know about what works for kids, I think I would." Unfortunately, she never came back to hear my speech about who is responsible for whose happiness. But I am not bashful about sharing it. It begins like this:

- My wife is not responsible for my happiness in the marriage.
- My congregation is not responsible for my happiness in the church.
- My bishop is not responsible for my happiness in the ministry.
- My mayor is not responsible for my happiness in the metropolis.
- Nor is my God responsible for my happiness in the universe.

But that's a digression. The point remains that two are better than one because they produce a better return. You can look it up.

Second, they also produce mutual assistance. "If they fall, one will lift up the other." That's what Ecclesiastes 4:10 says, before adding: "Woe to one who is alone and falls." The benefit being described is called "backstopping." Not backstabbing, but backstopping. And it is hard to live without it. If something gets past you or something gets to you, who backs you up? Who picks you up? I have been on the ground (because of both my stupidity and life's cruelty). And I have been reached for. Without such assistance, I might still be lying there.

Third, two are better than one because "if two lie together, they keep warm, but how can one keep warm alone?" Upon reading this, my first thought was of the time (a few winters back) when the power went off. It was off for several days. More to the point, it was off for several nights. Thank God for "bundling." But my second thought concerned the phrase "sleeping together" ... and the fact that kids have no way of understanding how much more there is to "sleeping together" than sex. When you sleep with someone for a long time, you know when something hurts her, haunts her, concerns her, or keeps her awake. You know when she has had a bad dream or is in pain. And you also know how incredibly close two people can be in a bed and how incredibly far apart they can also be in the same bed.

A friend lost his wife not long ago. She suffered for years before she died … suffered at home, alongside her husband. He has done all right since she died except at night in bed when he wakes up every two hours, because months before her death, she woke up every two hours. And as he heard her then, he hears her still.

Fourth, two are better than one because "though one might prevail against another, two will withstand one" against all kinds of enemies, including temptation.

Except for the first night, I chose to avoid the comings and strayings on that recent slice of "reality television" known as Temptation Island. I did have my secretary download the plot summaries from the Internet so I could keep in touch with everything that happened on the way to the see-all, tell-all finale. Most of you recall the format. Four couples were invited to a beautiful resort on a tropical island. In spite of previous commitments made to each other, the couples agreed to be separated and tempted to see if they would stay or stray. Most of the critics said this was "pure sleaze." But it was more than that. It was incredibly "painful sleaze." People were hurt. Even some of the unattached singles (gorgeous hunks of meat—male and female—who were there to provide the temptation) fell hard for the people they were trying to tempt. Which meant that they got bruised (where it did not show). Message being: "Even meat feels." Meanwhile, the producers said: "Trust us. We have taken every precaution against unsafe sex." My friends, when will we ever learn that there has never been a prophylactic big enough to cover the entirety of the human heart?

In summary, two are better than one—for work and warmth, and for assistance and resistance. Followed by "a threefold cord is not quickly broken."

Is the third strand God? The author does not say. So the scholars do not say, either. But I will. Because only when God is factored into the mix does marriage cease being an end in itself. You meet, and you date. You court, and you mate. You plan five years out. You plan ten years out. You plan thirty years out (fixed or adjustable), all the while asking, "Are we on track with our plan?" And pulse-taking. "Do you think we are doing as well as the other couples we know?" But the key to success may be riding a little looser in the saddle—looking up as well as in—while asking questions like:

- What is God giving to us?
- What is God doing through us?
- What is God asking of us?
- How is God's forgiveness working in us?

I guess I'm lucky. Or blessed. Maybe both. Go back with me to a Friday night dance in the fellowship hall of our church, where we had a great time with a nice mix of kids and adults. There was music by a teen band and talented DJ. Then the old clock on the wall said that we had reached 9:55—five minutes to closing. Teens, gone home. Families, gone home. Most everybody, gone home. A few of us tidying up in order to go home. The hall was dark, save for those little prism lights swirling on the floor. CDs still spinning. Slow stuff, now. Soft stuff, now. Mellow stuff, now. As the kids might have said, "Geezer music."

There were just a few of us on the floor—five couples, maybe six, none under 50—along with Anne Murray, the Canadian contralto who was crooning something a little bit this side of "country." It took a while to translate the rhythm from head to feet. What it was, was a waltz (one two three, one two three, one two three). Suddenly the feet remembered, which felt goodly and godly and more than a little romantic. After 35 years, can you believe it? Dancing in church, no less. With each other, no less. Close, no less. But what was Anne singing that made it all so special? She was singing, "Could I Have This Dance for the Rest of My Life?"

> *Would you be my partner, every night?*
> *When we're together, it feels so right.*

Epilogue: Kristine Ritter

Reflecting on Bill's words, "two are better than one," reminded me of a story I recently read about one of my ancestors. It appears that after the death of her husband, Friedrich Stempel, in 1749, his widow, Ann Stempel, remarried just ten months later. The writer noted that while this might be somewhat disrespectful today, in the eighteenth century, a woman had to marry for her physical survival and the survival of her children. Ann had at least four young children and was pregnant with another when her husband died. Two were not only better in the agricultural age, but economically, two were essential. Women today have many more choices, of course. They are quite capable of supporting themselves. They can support their children if they wish.

So why marry at all? Perhaps a recent German study can help us with some answers. This study reported remarkable benefits to husbands who kiss their wives each morning. They have fewer auto accidents and earn 20 to 30 percent more money. In addition, they are sick less and live an average of five years longer. Assuming that it is the close, warm relationship that enables "the kiss" to be something more than the mere pressing of lips, it appears that two are not only better than one but also can be:

Safer

Richer

Healthier

And longer living.

I remember my mother saying many years ago, "You've got to be able to work together; a good marriage is teamwork." Industry today is saying two (or four) are better than one. Today, effective teams are seen as a way to make better decisions and produce better quality products at a reasonable cost. Wouldn't this be a great objective for a marriage? Better quality at a reasonable cost? What makes a team successful? Team members who are committed to the goals and objectives of the team.

The data appears to support the premise of "two being better than one," but let me close not with data, but with a word of personal experience—35 years' worth of experience. Through deep pain and great joy, incredible demands on time and strength, memorable experiences and an involvement in something greater than myself, I would not have wanted to do it without my helpmate, soul mate, other half, and best friend. It has demanded all I could give and more, taught me more than I could ever have imagined, and I could never have done it alone.

First United Methodist Church
Birmingham, Michigan
2002

Note: A similar reference to "Could I Have This Dance for the Rest of My Life" appears earlier in this book. On that occasion, a different sermon was preached to a live congregation. On this occasion, the song is referenced in a published collection entitled, "Reflections on Marriage and Spiritual Growth," edited by Andrew Weaver and Carolyn Stapleton.

7

Yes

Scripture: II Corinthians 1:15-22

While commitment is the primary theme (and marriage the pivotal example) of this sermon, it was actually written for a congregation-wide finance campaign in 2004.

I do not know what the first audible word out of a child's mouth is likely to be. But I have watched parents attempt to coax, even bribe, their toddler into saying something that resembles "Mama" or "Dada." And, as in the game of horseshoes, close is usually good enough. "See, she said it," Mama exclaims to Dada ... even though Dada isn't sure he heard it (and Grandpa is absolutely certain he didn't hear it). But all of us know that what we want to hear goes a long way towards determining what we actually do hear. Which is why it is not uncommon for people to thank me profusely (at the door of the church) for having said so clearly something that I never said at all.

In thinking about the early speech of children, Kris and I tried to remember Julie's first word. But all that comes to mind is "ba" ... weeks and weeks of "ba." But since "ba" was usually delivered with one or more hands outstretched, I think it meant "I want it," or "Let me have it." And when the desired object was already within reach, it was clear to me that "ba" meant "more."

Just the other day, I overheard one of you say: "The good news is that my little girl has a new word which she speaks loudly and often. The bad news is that the word is "No." Later on, that word will come in handy ... if used, that is. We tell our teens "Just say no," fearful that they won't. By which we mean "no" to cigarettes ... "no" to beer ... "no" to boys (or to girls who, I am told, now make as many advances as boys, test the limits as often as boys, and push the edge of the sexual envelope as far as boys). And we especially hope they will say "no" to drugs. We applaud the teen who is able to say to the tempter: "Just what is it about the word 'no' you don't understand?"

Clearly, "no" is an early word ... a good word ... a self-defining, limit-setting, morality-maintaining word ... with much to commend it. But I would suggest that life is enriched and ultimately better served by the "yes" word. Because while "no" is off-putting, "yes" is in-viting. "No" separates. "Yes" embraces. In his classic little book on negotiation entitled *Getting to Yes: Negotiating Agreements Without Giving In*, Roger Fisher writes: "Every day families, neighbors, couples, employees, bosses, businesses, consumers, salespersons, lawyers, and nations face the same dilemma ... how to get to 'yes' without going to war."

I have said it so often that I now hear many of you quoting it back to me, that one of my cardinal rules of church administration is that (at every level of governance) we should strive to be a permission-giving rather than a permission-denying organization. Which, unfortunately, is not part of the DNA of most church bodies.

Picture the scene. A relative newcomer to a church (who could be a new member, but who could also be a new pastor) comes up with a wonderful idea for ministry ... or what he or she thinks would be a wonderful idea for ministry. Only to be told: "Before you go off half-cocked, you'd better test that out with the committee ... the council ... the board ... the trustees." Who, in their collective wisdom, listen to it ... ponder it ... table it ... come back to it ... pro it and con it ... then kick it around and around and around and around until most of the passion leaks out of it ... never completely condemning it ... but saying in response to it:

- We've already tried it.

- Where would we find the money for it?

- Where would we find the people for it?

- Where would we find the room for it?

- Has anybody asked the lawyers what our liabilities might be, were we to attempt it?

- And, all things considered, wouldn't next year be a better time for it?

To which I have consistently countered: "The primary function of governance is to encourage, underwrite, publicize, and then get out of the way so that stuff can happen. If it is a good idea, the people will be there. And if God is in the idea, the money will be there."

Last Wednesday night at the Trustees meeting, a letter was shared, written by Jeff Nelson. Jeff was proposing that there be not one, but two senior high mission trips next spring. Different parts of the country (Mexico and Memphis). Different sized groups. Different objectives. But both trips were well thought out and researched. At issue was what role, if any, the Trustees would play in funding these ventures, given that among the smaller endowments the Trustees control is one committed to the support of youth ministry.

Given prior experience, the Trustees had a formula for funding one trip. But not for two. So I sat there in amazement and watched them do a little creative financing that would allow them to double the amount, rather than simply splitting the amount. Which wasn't hard, especially after one of them said: "After all, isn't our challenge to find ways to grant rather than withhold permission?" After which he then said: "And having just received my Steeple Notes, didn't I read where the title of our pastor's sermon for this Sunday is 'Yes'?" Which was when I thought to myself, how many of my colleagues spend their entire ministries without ever, even once, experiencing the grace of God at a meeting of the Board of Trustees?

But the word "yes" defines persons every bit as much as it defines institutions. Let me illustrate with a story I have told to countless new member classes, but never (to my knowledge) from this pulpit. Several years ago, a fellow asked a question at a new member orientation that I couldn't answer ... or at least, that I didn't answer very well. Said he:

> Bill, I like your church. (Not that it was, or is, my
> church, but you'd be surprised how many people refer to
> it that way. Note to clergy who think that people can be
> trained to think differently about whose church it is:
> they can't, so you might as well give it up.)

> I like your church (he said). But I've picked up on
> something in the months I've been coming here. When I
> look around at all the things your church has to offer, it
> seems as if I can do any of them ... even all of them ...

whether I'm a member or not. So given that I am more
the loner-type than the member-type, why should I join?

And he was right, of course. There wasn't much he couldn't do as a non-member that would suddenly be open to him if he became a member. As a non-member, he could worship in the sanctuary … sing in the choir … attend any class … teach any class … serve on any committee … attend any function … counsel the youth … join a baseball team … or go on a mission trip. In addition, he could have his baby baptized here, his daughter married here, his Uncle Louie buried here, and no one would ever deny him the Sacrament of the Lord's Supper here. Moreover, we would gladly (and without reservation) take his money here.

As a non-member, among the few things denied him would be the opportunity to vote on a capital project, serve as chair of the Board of Trustees, or become president of the United Methodist Women. But in all my years of teaching new member classes, I have yet to meet anyone whose primary question was: "How can I become president of the United Methodist Women?" In terms of privileges granted versus privileges denied, there is little or no advantage in becoming a member of any United Methodist church … at least not as the world defines the word "advantage."

Which was when I remembered Peter's question of Jesus, again concerning advantages: "Lord, if we stay, what's in it for us?" But I didn't tell this guy about the cross (which was what was "in it" for Jesus) or the cruel deaths (that were "in it" for several followers of Jesus). In truth, I don't remember what I said to the guy. But I know what I've said to others since. I've told them various versions of the following story. Indulge me.

The date is July 2, 1966. It's about 3:05 in the afternoon. I am standing at the intersection of two carpeted aisles. There are three in tuxedos behind me ... three in tea-length formals across from me ... and two in black robes perched one step above me. Rising to their feet at the swelling of the organ, it feels like there are five thousand to the left of me and five thousand to the right of me. And there, walking toward me, down the center aisle of First Methodist Church of Dearborn, was the lovely Kristine Larson of Novi. And as she got closer and closer ... and my collar got tighter and tighter ... and my stomach, queasier and queasier ... and my eyes, moister and moister ... I thought to myself: "This isn't just hanging around with Tina Larson anymore."

Which realization was followed by my "Yes" to her and her "Yes" to me, cemented in phrases about better/worse, richer/poorer and sickness/health. So was I ready for that? Probably. But did I even remotely grasp the implications of that? Probably not. Though it occurred to me some years later that that "yes" ... spoken that day ... to that woman ... has made all the difference in my life. But more than that, it has been all the "yeses," spoken on all the other days, that have made all the difference in my life. I am talking about yeses to a pair of schools ... a pair of children ... a quartet of churches ... a bevy of bishops ... and one very inquisitive board of ministerial inquiry. But I could just as well be talking about yeses to friends and family, tasks and travels. I owe my life to a slew of yeses.

The funny thing is, I have long since forgotten the "nos" ... jobs I've turned down ... females I've turned down ... invitations I declined ... schools I rejected ... roads I traveled not. Speculation concerning what might have been is just that ... speculation. But the "yeses" have meant commitments. And it is the commitments that have made all the difference. Void of the commitments, my life would be an empty shell of what it is today.

All of which is capstoned by my commitment to Jesus Christ. Some years ago, Dag Hammarskjold, the Secretary-General of the United Nations and winner of the Nobel Peace Prize in 1961 (who lost his life on a peacekeeping mission in a plane crash over the Congo), wrote:

> *"I don't know who, or what put the question.*
> *I don't know when it was put.*
> *I don't even remember answering.*
> *But at some moment, I did answer, "Yes"*
> *to someone/something.*

> *And from that hour, I was certain that existence was*

meaningful, and that life ... my life, lived in self-surrender ... had a goal."

From a very early time in my life, I knew a question had been put. And while I can't pinpoint one specific moment that might be called "The Ask" ... or another specific moment that might be called "The Answer" ... I knew that Jesus Christ was at the heart of both "The Ask" and "The Answer" ... and that anything other than a "yes" would have relegated me to a life that was less.

But none of those were the ultimate "yes." Those were simply "yeses" said by me. Which, while important, paled before the "yes" that was said to me.

In our text, Paul is in trouble. Again. Having rearranged his travel plans so as to put off (for a time) his promise to return to Corinth, his detractors (of whom there were many) said: "First he says yes. Then he says no. What should we believe? Is it yes or is it no? And if there is nothing about his promises we can take to the bank, how can we trust the things he has told us about the promises of God? Maybe God is as fickle as Paul is."

To which Paul does three things. First, he defends his integrity (my "yes" is good). Second, he defends his theology (God's "yes" is good). Finally, he puts the entire matter into a most vivid phrase: "Jesus is the 'yes' to every promise of God."

So, assuming you believe that, let me ask you what you think. Will God turn back … turn away … turn his heart … or turn tail and run? Will God sour on us … quit on us … walk away from us … or wash his hands and say "To hell with us"? Will God let us stew in our juice … slosh in our slime … sink in our sin … or stink in our playpen? Will God hand us over to our multiple enemies without a fight … turning off (once and for all) the spigot from "whence the healing stream doth flow?"

"No," says Paul to the Romans. We shall be more than conquerors … think about that, "more" than conquerors … through him who loved us. Jesus, being the "yes" to every promise of God. Then, as Paul goes on to say in verse 22: "The Holy Spirit in our hearts constitutes the earnest money (Greek word "arrabon") or the first installment paid on that guarantee."

Don't you see what that means? The "yes" has already been spoken. If only the church could hear that. If only those churches that love the sound of the word "no" could believe that. Says the world to the church: "Your lips tell me no, no … but there's yes, yes in your eyes." Thankfully, in some corners of Christendom, the ayes still have it.

Note: This sermon was preached on Ingathering Sunday, when congregants bring both their offerings for the current year and their pledges of support for the coming year.

As to Roger Fisher's book, "Getting to Yes", I can't say that I have read it. But I have seen it quoted in other places, most recently by Peter Gomes of Harvard. Dag Hammarskjold's quote comes from his highly acclaimed memoir, Markings.

First United Methodist Church
Birmingham, Michigan
November 14, 2004

8

Letting Go

Scripture: Ruth 1:6-18

These words, raw with an emotion all parents understand, were written and delivered less than 48 hours after delivering our daughter, Julie, to her freshman year at Duke University.

A couple of weeks ago, when I was cross-checking calendars with my running partner, Dick Cheatham, I reminded him that I would have to miss our next scheduled workout, given the trip that Kris and I were making to deliver Julie to her first year at Duke. This was not unfamiliar conversational terrain between Dick and myself. As good friends do, we had discussed both the facts of her move and our feelings surrounding the move. Which is, perhaps, what led Dick to remark, as a parting word:

"I hope you do better than I did when Diane and I took Crystal to Michigan State. I kissed her goodbye, turned my back, bit my lip, and cried all the way home. But since Crystal's dorm was in East Lansing and our home (at that time) was in Brighton, "all the way home" only represented 30 minutes of tears. If you cry all the way home from Duke, you'll be red-eyed for 12 hours, 700 miles, and become something of a public menace on the highways."

I am here to report that I did nothing of the kind. Kris and I took her ... unloaded her ... spent a couple of days with her ... oriented her ... kissed her goodbye ... and drove away. In the immediate aftermath, there were a couple of sniffles and some long, introspective silences. Then Kris and I engaged in an extensive rehash of three very tightly-scheduled and emotionally-laden days. I don't know everything Kris may have been thinking. But I was certain that I was doing well. That was Friday morning.

Much of Friday afternoon was spent driving through the residual rain squalls of Hurricane Andrew. It was tense driving ... tough driving ... white-knuckled, rigid-necked, through the mountains driving. Then (somewhere around Pittsburgh) when the heavens finally decided to stop weeping, I started. Which launched Kris. And for the next 30 minutes, there was little either of us could say that made it any easier, or any better. So we just held hands or touched each other's leg, doing anything to make a connection, and (secondarily) to make it down the highway.

All in all, Julie couldn't be happier with her choice. And we couldn't be happier for her. After a Thursday filled with separate orientation activities for parents and freshmen, and after her first full night in the dorm, we picked her up for one final breakfast at our hotel. She was operating on four hours of sleep, having socialized with newly made friends until 3:00 in the morning. Still, she was vibrantly awake, bubbling over about her classes, her classmates, her room, and everything from the way the place looked to the way the place felt. "This is even better than I expected," she pronounced. "This feels exactly like where I should be."

Which makes it easy for us to be happy for her ... and easier to leave her. A ton of work went into the making of this decision, and early confirmation of its rightness, however premature, felt good. May future pulse-takings be so healthy and feel so fine. It could have been so much worse, and then our sadness would have had a real "bite" to it.

As it was, a tear or two was as predictable as it was explainable. She is our last kid. She is a "neat" kid. And 700 miles is not an easily-negotiable distance for any kid. She has not only gone away, but she has gone a very long way, away. Whatever else Duke may be, it is not a "commuter college" for people who live in Michigan.

As parents go, Kris and I may be an overly sentimental pair.

Although I think not. More honest about our emotions, perhaps, but not more emotional. I think that such things are "big deals" for a lot of you. And unless I miss my bet, a number of you are going to tell me so at the close of the hour.

In the orientation session for parents, we heard from three different speakers, with each speaker zeroing in on the issue of "separation anxiety." Not class schedules. Not dormitory regulations. Not grading procedures, health services or financial aid. But separation anxiety. "This is a major transition," we were told. "It is hard for them. It is equally hard for you." Such was the tone of the messages. And I

Bill enjoys a Duke football game with Julie, 1995

thought to myself: "How perceptive. How 'right on." Because this was what we all were dealing with. Not with, "Where can my kid stash her bicycle?" or "How does my kid get a lock on her closet?" But: "How am I going to leave my kid here and go home … when I am not all that ready to leave my kid here or go home?" As to what the kids may have been thinking (listening to similar presentations elsewhere) heaven only knows. But given my ability to read crowds, it was clear that the people speaking to us were touching all the right buttons and hitting all the right nerves.

Not that they did it without humor. Separation anxiety can be pretty heavy stuff, unbroken by levity. One speaker told us that she knew why God created adolescence: "So that when our kids are ready to go to college, we are ready to have them go." Other speakers listed some of the immediate "pluses" we would experience, especially if we were saying goodbye to the last one. Such pluses included no more MTV … fewer wet towels on the bathroom floor … the possibility of refrigerated leftovers actually being left over … and the sheer delight of hearing the phone ring and knowing that possibly, just possibly, it might be for you.

We were reminded that, as parents, we were still very much needed. We would get urgent phone calls of three distinct types.

- requests for sustenance: "I have overspent my Duke account and have less than $20 in my checkbook."

- requests for encouragement: "I have never had less than a "B" in my life, and now I haven't gotten above a "C" on my last three papers."

- requests for advice: "I've forgotten everything I ever knew about washing underwear. Tell me again, where is it you're supposed to insert the quarter?"

Therefore, Kris and I have little doubt that we will be needed, valued, and that our parenting chores are far from finished. Yet, there was also little doubt in either of our minds that the single most important parenting chore we could do at that particular moment was to go home ... without trying to fix, correct, amend, or teach one more thing. "Just go home," making as small a deal out of the whole matter as possible. Not because going home is really a "small deal." But because going home is such an incredibly "big deal" that it is (for many) almost too hot to handle and too close to touch.

Julie is one of those rare kids who talks about virtually everything and anything with us. Yet even she said: " We'll be okay as long as nobody tries to make any speeches." So none of us did. Kris spent the final pre-departure days helping Julie assemble her stuff. And at Julie's request, I took her to the Whitney for a final daddy-daughter lunch. (Seven years earlier, Bill's choice had been the London Chop House. Whatever else my kids may lack, you can't say they don't have class). But there were no speeches. Had she asked me, I simply would have said: "Julie, whether by planning, providence or accident, you seem to have stumbled on an amazingly successful formula for living your life. Don't abandon it now," And I believe that she's heard that … and that she knows that … without my needing to put it in a final "speech" at all.

"There is a time to embrace, and a time to refrain from embracing." So said a wise old biblical sage writing under the pen name "Ecclesiastes." If you stretch that a bit, I suppose it also means that for every time of holding close, there is also a time of letting go. Among the many things love does, love releases. Virtually every Sunday morning, given the location of my office, I see a parent struggling with what it means to walk away from a screaming, clinging toddler in the nursery. And while I know how hard that is, I know how necessary it is. And I also know that the same scene sometimes repeats itself at the other end of life's spectrum. I see love occasionally expressed in the words of one family member saying to another: "I am going to miss you terribly, but it's ok for you to go." Lots of people are simply are unable to die until they've been given permission. Love releases.

Earlier, I read to you a portion of Ruth's story. It is located in the one part of the Old Testament that most people can manage, which is probably why it's one part of the Old Testament that people love. But when you look at it, it is just as much Naomi's story as it is Ruth's. Naomi is a Jew, married to Elimelech, another Jew. They have a pair of sons. The sons grow up. A famine hits the land. Naomi, her husband,

and her two sons move to Moab ... a foreign country. Moab has food. Moab has jobs. Moab also has women. Each of Naomi's sons marry Moabite women. One marries Orpah (that's Orpah, not Oprah). The other marries Ruth. Then things take a turn for the worse. Naomi's husband dies, followed by each of her sons. Just like that. All the men are gone. Naomi is left with a pair of foreign women for daughters-in-law. Naomi decides to go back to Israel. But realizing that Israel is no place for a pair of young, attractive, non-Jewish widows, Naomi tells them: "Split. Make your home here. Among your own people. I'm going home. To be with my people. Your chances of finding husbands in Israel are two ... slim and none. You'll do better here. People know you here. People worship like you do, here. Even if I get married ... get pregnant ... and get two more sons ... by the time they'd be grown up, you'd have callouses on your hope chests."

To which Orpah says: "Makes sense to me. Here, let me kiss you good-bye, mommy-in-law dearest." And to which Ruth says (while clinging fervently to Naomi):

> *Entreat me not to leave thee,*
> *For whether thou goest, I will go.*
> *Whither thou lodgest, I will lodge,*
> *Thy people will be my people,*
> *And thy God, my God.*

Now everybody loves those lines, especially when they read them (as I did) from the stilted prose of the King James Version of the Bible. And everybody, upon reading them, looks at Ruth and says: "What devotion. What love. What fidelity to Naomi. And she's not even her daughter, save by marriage."

But Naomi, however grateful she may be for Ruth's companionship, realizes that this is not as it should be. Ruth should have a life of her own ... lived on her own ... in response to commitments made on her own. So, in the part of the story nobody ever quotes, Naomi orchestrates a scenario wherein Ruth meets a rich, eligible, Jewish bachelor, whereupon she marries him and bears his children (one of whom becomes the grandfather of King David). In an even less quoted part of the story, Naomi teaches Ruth some tactics in the gentle art of flirtation (in reality, the gentle art of seduction) so as to insure that Ruth will get her man.

It appears that the Jews have preserved this story for a whole host of reasons, including whatever light it may have shed on the changing practice of interfaith marriage. After all, if King David's great-grandmother was a foreigner ... and a seducer of David's great-grandfather (who, incidentally, was half in the bag when Ruth first came to lie at his feet) ... it shoots a pretty big hole in the notion of ethnic superiority and racial purity on the part of the Jewish people. Right?

But not to be lost is this elemental understanding of Naomi, who (in effect) says to Ruth: "As much as I love you ... and as much as I need you ... you need to be on with your life. And if you will not take that step on your own (however admirable that devotion may be), I will have to take it for you." Which is what Naomi did (perhaps to her own short-term detriment, but to the long-term betterment of Ruth).

Love lets go. And it sometimes falls to those of us who are older to instigate the release. Not to be overlooked (in life) is the subtle ministry of the gentle nudge.

I am sure this was painful for Naomi, not solely because of what she may have feared for Ruth, but because of what she may have feared for herself. Separation anxiety is always harder on the one doing the releasing than it is on the one being released. Which is another new truth I discovered over the course of the last five days. When Naomi said to Ruth, "Don't look to my womb to produce you a new husband," what she was really saying was:

> *Time marches on.*
> *Human beings get older.*
> *I'm getting older.*
> *And some things will never be the same again.*

I know the feeling. During the last few of my child-raising years, people have said to me: "Treasure these days with your kids. They go by so incredibly quickly." I always listened and nodded, figuring that what they meant was that kids get old before you know it. It never occurred to me that what they meant was that I would get old before I knew it. A few minutes before we left home last Tuesday (practical parent that I am), I decided to walk through the entire house in search of potentially forgotten items. In the basement, I found a portable electric fan. Necessity! In the basement, I also found a child's table and chairs along with several Barbies. No longer necessities! I remembered buying every last one of them and felt suddenly sad. It also took me a few minutes to come up from the basement.

I'm going to be all right. We are going to be all right. I say "we" because that's where it rests now ... with the two of us. Which may be why Kris and I felt a need to touch each other a lot on the way home (especially during those miles when we couldn't say anything without breaking into tears). A line from an old Sonny Bono song kept creeping into consciousness ... "Just you and me, babe."

And Julie will be all right, too ... although I can't ensure, determine or guarantee that. Would that I could. All I can do is trust. Trust who she is ... what Kris has done ... what I have done ... what others have done ... and what God will do. But even trust has its risks.

I prayed to God and said: "Don't let her fall, God. Don't let her fail. Don't let her meet up with anyone who'll abuse her, hurt her, or disappoint her. She is my little girl. Do you know what it feels like to be a father?"

And God, who still occasionally speaks with a hint of a Jewish accent, said: "Do I know vat it means to be a father? You got a minute? Sit down ... let me tell you about my boy ..."

Nardin Park United Methodist Church
Farmington Hills, Michigan
August 30, 1992

9

Update From the Valley

Scripture: Deuteronomy 33:26-29, Psalm 23

What follows was written and delivered 14 months after the suicide of our first born son, Bill. It subsequently appeared in a book of sermons by this author, "Take the Dimness of My Soul Away: Healing After a Loved One's Suicide."

Letter to the Congregation

Dear First Church Friends:

Beloved United Methodist scholar, Dr. Albert Outler, left behind an admirable body of scholarly work in the fields of church history and theology. He also left a number of sermons to testify that scholars can speak with deep personal insight and empathy. In one such sermon, he moved from a discussion of the trials and tribulations of greater Dallas to some more personal observations of the neighborhood he knew best.

> *Mrs. Outler and I live in a quiet, peaceable*
> *neighborhood, and we take long walk-talks in our five-*
> *block area almost daily. Over the years we have come to*
> *know many of our neighbors. And the better we get to*
> *know any one family, the more we learn of the tragic*
> *admixture of human happiness and wretchedness in a*
> *setting that looks as if it were as favorable an*
> *environment as one could find. There is not a single*
> *family in our area, as far as we know them, without its*
> *share of heartbreak.*

Having worked in some extremely "favorable" human environments, I know he is right. I have seen the world's pain behind even the most ornate of doors. And, as a family, we Ritters have had occasion to taste a bit of it ourselves. More or less widely known is the fact that our firstborn son, Bill, Jr., died on May 2, 1994, of his own hand. In response to which I have shared one previous sermon ("When the Bough Breaks," delivered on May 29, 1994). Many of you claim you can see traces of the impact elsewhere in my preaching, even though the specifics of Bill's death are not mentioned.

This is, I suppose, to the good. While each of us retains an essential quotient of privacy, there is no need to hide the things that touch us deeply. Neither, in my case, would such be possible. We are an incredibly public family. Much about our lives reads like an "open book." Following last year's Memorial Day sermon, Kris and I drove to our getaway home on Grand Traverse Bay. While motoring north, I realized that the only people "out of the loop" about Bill's death were my Elk Rapids neighbors. Later that same afternoon, I made my rounds, door to door, to the ones I knew best. My neighbor to the south was my first stop. Despite eight years of a shared lot line, I couldn't say I knew him well. Our talk had consisted mostly of shrubs, trees and lake levels. So you can imagine my surprise in learning that his son's life had ended similarly, nine years earlier. Deep into the conversation, I heard myself say: "Tell me when it stops hurting." To which he said: "If it ever does, I'll let you know." Then he went on to add that, while everything had changed, some things had healed, and I would grow both through (and from) the experience.

He was right. On both counts. The pain has not gone away. But I have grown. And learned. Although the truths have come hard. For while there is much in books and pamphlets about grieving, none of it speaks exactly to me, or about me.

Now it is time to return to the subject sermonically. Why? Several reasons. First, because I said I would. Second, because some of the benchmarks of my journey have already proved helpful to others. Third, because I am one who doesn't always know what I think until I hear myself say it. St. Augustine once wrote: "I write in order to know what I think." Which is probably why painters paint, singers sing, and poets ponder the mysteries of human existence. The sermon is entitled "An Update From the Valley." The very nature of the title should imply that this is far from a finished process. But I have found a secure enough place to stand so as to be able to report what … and who … I see.

Sincerely,

William A. Ritter

The Sermon

It hardly seems that six days have gone by, given all that has happened since Monday. The place was Elk Rapids. The time was 9:00 in the morning. The day was dressed with sunshine. And I was dressed for golf. When the call came, telling me that Bruce Duncan committed suicide at the all-too-early age of 31.

Bruce's parents are our friends. Bruce's father, Ed, is my colleague. We went to Yale together. We came to Michigan together. We served over 30 years in Methodist churches together. Ed officiated at our wedding (when our hearts were young and gay) and helped us bury our son (when they were less so). Unlike Bill, Jr., who was our first born, Bruce was their last. A studious and sensitive young man, Bruce completed his work at the New Haven Public Library on Friday, withdrew the balance of his bank account in a check made payable to his parents, shared a comfortable evening with friends, and sometime Saturday set out for northern Michigan and the town of Frankfort, to which his parents had retired seven weeks ago. Motoring through Ohio, he stopped and bought a gun. Then he continued until he stopped again, 30 miles from home. After leaving his car by the side of the road, he walked into the woods and didn't come out.

Kris and I visited his family on Monday … attended to the details of getting pulpit robe and dress clothes from Birmingham to Elk Rapids on Tuesday … and I preached his funeral in Frankfort on Friday. It was 51 weeks to the day since Ed accompanied us to Oakland Hills Cemetery in Novi for the purpose of interring young Bill's ashes in Kris' family plot. Ed confessed, at the time, that he hoped our roles in this sad and tragic drama would never be reversed. He was wrong. They were.

All last week, people said to us: "Surely this will reopen old wounds." Which it did. Not that the scar tissue covering the "old wounds" was all that thick. But Bruce's death brought it all back … from hearing the awful truth to facing an awful death. Already this summer, two other people we know tried the same thing and succeeded. While another tried the same thing and failed. Interesting, isn't it, that suicide is the one activity where success is failure and failure is success. The representative of the Farmington Hills police department who came to deliver the sad news of Bill, closed my office door and simply said: "Reverend Ritter, it is my sad duty to report to you that sometime late last night or early this morning, your son completed a successful suicide." Reflecting on his words, I found myself thinking: "If only Bill could have failed."

But as I said, Bruce's death brought the pain back. Not that it had far to travel. Pat Conroy's long awaited novel, *Beach Music*, begins with a beautiful young wife and mother jumping from a South Carolina bridge. Conroy describes the scene with these lines:

> *As Shyla steadied herself on the rail, a man approached*
> *her from behind ... a man up from Florida besotted with*
> *the intoxicating combination of citrus and Disney ...*
> *and said in a low voice, so as not to frighten the comely*
> *stranger on the bridge: "Are you okay, honey?"*

> *She pirouetted and faced him. Then, with tears*
> *trailing down her face, she stepped back. And with that*
> *step, changed the lives of our family forever.*

Is that too dramatic? I think not.

I have spent much of my life observing death and dying from a front row seat ... close enough to get my feet (and sometimes my face) wet with the feelings of others. That's because death hurts. All death hurts. Even kindly death ... friendly death ... prayed-for death ... and death that is said to come as a "blessing." It all hurts. So I do not pretend, even for a moment, that what happened to us is necessarily worse than what has happened to you. Such comparisons get us nowhere.

Yet, I have learned (from people who know more about these things than I do) that recovery is made measurably more difficult when any one of five factors is present. Those factors include:

> When death takes someone young.
>
> When death takes someone unexpectedly.
>
> When death takes someone suddenly.
>
> When death takes someone violently.
>
> When death is self-inflicted.

You do the math. When you add 'em up, we've had all five.

Still, Kris and I had to start somewhere. And we did not lack for words of advice, many of which proved to be abundantly helpful. Let me recount (and briefly comment upon) three such advisements.

First, we were told to actualize Bill's death. Don't dwell on it. But don't dodge it, either. Go back through it. Probe the questions. Sort the papers. Secure the autopsy results. Read the police reports. Talk to Bill's friends. Go through Bill's things. Sift through the final days and hours of Bill's life.

There is no end to the people who will step forward to do that stuff for you. Their aim is to spare you. And it is a good aim. But it is not always on target. Some things you need to do for you. And "getting in touch with what has happened" is one of them.

To be sure, there are limits to each individual's comfort zone. I am not suggesting that you violate yours. But there is some value in pushing against it. My friend Ed went quickly to the site of Bruce's death, the better to see it for himself. Then he went to view Bruce's body. In my case, I was advised against doing the latter. So I didn't. Now I wish I had. But how was I to know I would eventually regret not having done so?

Searching through it all, I thought I would find something that would surprise me … a clue … a conversation … a missing puzzle piece … a fresh slice of information. But I didn't. From day one, I had a pretty good working knowledge of the factors that contributed to Bill's decision. Yet I kept thinking I would stumble upon something more … something that would enable his death to make sense (as I define "sense"), rather than as Bill defined it in his last days and hours. But it is the nature of suicide that it will never make the kind of sense to me as it somehow made to him. This is why I keep returning to George Buttrick's line: "Life is essentially a series of events to be borne and lived through, rather than a series of riddles to be played with and solved." Which means that in coming to terms with sorrow, courage counts for a whole lot more than brilliance.

All we really know is that suicide is usually undertaken as an antidote to pain. Which caused my friend Ed to say, last Monday afternoon: "As much as I hurt for me, I hurt even more for Bruce ... and what he must have felt." For such pain has a strangely malignant quality, so that even if we could find and isolate the lesion of origin, there is no way to go back and excise it in retrospect. Death's valley casts its shadow, even before death itself does. And it is a darkening shadow. Moments ago we sang the powerful words of George Croly's hymn, "Spirit of God, Descend Upon My Heart." Don't miss the lament that is threaded through the second verse.

> *I ask no dream, no prophet ecstasies.*
> *No sudden rending of the veil of clay.*
> *No angel visitant, no opening skies,*

Which is then followed by the plea:

> *Just take the dimness of my soul away.*

Translated, that means: "I am not asking you to light up my sky, O Lord. Just find some way to keep the 'gray' that is coloring my world from becoming terminal."

But what happens when you open the crayon box and "gray" is the only color there is? What happens when the best efforts of family and friends can't recolor your world? And what happens when the fire that once warmed your heart grows cold, until the light that once illumined your future goes out? Dimness of soul. That's what happens. To the point that it sometimes costs you your life.

As for the second piece of advice, we were told: "Don't blame yourself." So easy to say. So hard to do. We kept asking ourselves, What could we have done? What should we have done? What didn't we do? To which one answer was: "You did plenty. And then some. Everybody says so." In point of fact, Bill said so.

Yet guilt is there. That's because it grows, as every parent knows, out of the myth of our own omnipotence. As if we really could make it all go right ... or go away ... for our children. It starts early in the parenting process, this omnipotence myth. Your child cries out in the night. And even though you can sleep through anything else, you hear that cry. You know that cry. You go to that cry. And whether that cry is occasioned by a nightmare or an ear infection, your response is always the same. You touch your child ... hold your child ... cradle your child ... even as you hear yourself saying: "There, there, it's going to be all right." And you say that, even though you don't know that. You say that, even though there will come a night with a cry you can't answer ... a problem you can't fix ... a pain you can't remedy. You will not be able to go through life making everything "all right," even though you won't be able to shake the feeling that you should. And so forgiveness, when (and if) you finally give it to yourself, is not so much for anything you did or didn't do, but for the fact that (at some critical juncture) you were merely human.

The third piece of advice sounded paradoxical and required something of a balancing act to achieve. "Keep busy," we were told. "But take time." I chose to over-focus on the first part. I kept busy. I raced back to work. I did a funeral in ten days, two weddings in two weeks, and a sermon in three. Some of which was clearly avoidance. Not denial. Avoidance. There is a difference. Denial means saying it didn't happen … acting as if it didn't happen … and pretending it didn't happen. Avoidance knows full well it happened, but attempts to bracket the pain and put it on the shelf for later.

I feared that if I didn't re-normalize things quickly, my life would never be normal. When people said, "This will take years," they were trying to be kind. But I cringed every time I heard it. The thought that it might take years was so frightening and intolerable; I was determined I wasn't even going to give it months. I decided I would speed the process, even force-feed the process. Which I did. By sheer heroic effort.

Part of that is simply me. One grieves as one lives. And I am the kind of person who gets over things by plowing through them. Even though I have never lived on a farm, a plow is an appropriate image … work-related, labor-intensive and forward-focused. That's me. That's either who I am, or so closely related to my self-perception so as to be inseparable from who I am. I once described myself as the Walt Terrell of the ministry. Some of you remember Walt Terrell. He used to pitch for the Tigers. Sparky Anderson liked him. A lot. That's because

Sparky said: "Every fourth day you just hand Walter the baseball and he goes out and throws it. He may not always throw it successfully. He may not always throw it brilliantly. But when you hand it to him, he never turns it down."

Which is how I approached my work. Except that my work is not just any work. My work is unique, in that much of it is done for others. I could preach a funeral ten days after Bill died … along with Bruce's funeral on Friday that looked like it could have been Bill's funeral all over again … because there were people who needed what I could do for them, more than I needed not to do it. It's Gospel Economics 101. You get back by puttin' out.

Still, there are limits to the "work is therapy" school of grief management. And I reached them. Several people said to me last summer: "After Bill died, we thought you'd take a month and sit by your lake." Which would have driven me crazy at the time. But which is not without appeal now. One gets tired. If not from work, one gets tired from trying to keep too many feelings on too high a shelf for too long a time. But hold that thought. I'll return to it in a minute.

Before I do, let me append a trio of other words.

ABOUT SURVIVAL! We are doing it. Surviving, that is. A year has passed … and then some. I am smart enough to put no stock in timetables. You shouldn't, either. But we feel good to have reached this one with our marriage intact, our health intact, our jobs intact, Julie's grades intact and our faith intact. Not everybody is so fortunate. When I read of how many others find their losses compounded, I feel good about being where we are. Several weeks ago, a couple came to see me, one week after their son's suicide. They were of a similar age, telling a similar story. I didn't know them. I'd never met them. Still, I spent an hour and a half with them. And I hadn't the foggiest idea if I'd helped them. But I went home and told Kris: "Their words were hard to hear, but good to hear. For while I can remember being where they are, I am not there now." And that was the first time I gave myself any points for having gained some ground.

Valleys are long ... and deep ... and wide. But not every acre of the valley is equally thick or equally dark. What's more, valleys are bisected by roads. To be sure, few of them are freeways. But they are traversable. And some are graded.

ABOUT FRIENDS! What more can we say? Without friends, we might not make it. It's that basic. I continue to marvel that people who claimed they didn't know what to do or say, did both so magnificently. Where did they all come from? Interesting, isn't it, that the phrase "Whatever did we do to deserve this?" can (on one day) express so much anguish, and (on the next day) so much gratitude. Thank you. Thank you. For more than occasionally smiling upon us with the face of Christ.

ABOUT THEOLOGY! On Friday, I said to a room filled with preachers:

> Some will say God had a reason for this. Others will add that God's wisdom is greater than our wisdom ... that God's thoughts are not our thoughts ... that God's ways are unsearchable. But I am not one who has ever been content to settle or be satisfied there. Borrowing the well-traveled words of Bill Coffin, I think that when Bruce got out of that car in Mesick, walked into the woods and never came out, God's heart was the first of hundreds to break.

> Fortunately, it has always been my conviction that while there may be some pain that God can't explain, there is no pain that God can't embrace.

Which brings me to the loose end I dangled earlier (when I was talking about work ... time ... and the need to feel what must be felt, in the midst of doing what must be done).

Earlier this summer, when I made my first trip to Elk Rapids, I preceded Kris and Julie by a few days. The excuse I gave myself was a backlog of chores. But the real reason was to spend some time by myself. One evening, at dusk, I was sitting on my deck ... reading ... thinking ... looking at the water ... letting my mind drift. When suddenly I found myself thinking about little kids. Mine. Yours. Anybody's. And how they like to test themselves by jumping from high places. There they are, standing on the edge of a sofa … straddling a fence post … perched on a step ladder or garage roof. Their knees,

Bill Ritter Jr., 1993

bent. Their shoulders, hunched. They appear poised and ready to jump. Except they do not jump. Or they do not jump until they first capture your eye (and your ear). "Catch me, daddy," is what they say. "Come over here and catch me when I jump." And you move closer, preparing to do just that. So they do. And you do. All things considered, it's a rather remarkable arrangement.

But what if there comes a day when they jump and you can't catch them? Because your arms aren't long enough … strong enough … quick enough … or near enough. When my friend Ed described walking into the woods with his daughter, he said a most interesting thing: "We were able to see where Bruce fell." But the tragedy consists of the fact that they weren't able to stop Bruce from falling.

•••••••

I couldn't catch Bill, either. But then again, he didn't tell me he was going to jump. Neither did he wait for me to get my arms in position. Thinking about this on my deck at sunset, I cried and cried. Then I looked down at my book and saw the verse from Deuteronomy that had triggered this line of thinking in the first place.

The eternal God is your dwelling place, and underneath are the everlasting arms.

And I realized that though I missed Bill (in that I failed to catch him) … and continue to miss Bill (in that I no longer have him) … my arms are not the only arms … and my arms are not the final arms. Which means that where he fell is not where he lays.

First United Methodist Church
Birmingham, Michigan
August 13, 1995

10

Chutes and Ladders, Revisited

Scripture: Ecclesiastes 9:7-12 and Philippians 4:10-20

Having already read about the day that we took Julie to Duke ("Letting Go"), I invite you to read what I wrote for the Sunday morning after Julie's Harvard graduation.

I've been to Boston (as the song says). Plenty of reason to go before. Very little reason to go again. For the kid is done ... with Harvard, I mean. MBA behind her. Job in California before her. Proud parents beside her.

Graduation was wonderful ... and wet. Ten minutes into the outdoor ceremony, the heavens opened, and it poured. Leading one parent to proclaim: " ... it's not enough that they soak you for tuition ..." Fortunately, I took two suits. Kris took two dresses. And between us, we took two hearts ... both of them bursting with pride. For while the day couldn't have dawned any worse, her future couldn't look any brighter.

Actually, graduation was three days' worth of events. There were dinners and parties and receptions. Having met Julie's friends on previous visits, we now met her friends' families on this visit. And they met us, with all of the attendant telling of stories and sharing of histories. One of the stories even merited national attention.

Graduating from business school with Julie was Cheryl Kozlowski, whose family was no less proud of her than we were of Julie. Except that on what should have been Cheryl's day in the sun, it was her dad who commanded the headlines, given that 24 hours before his daughter's graduation, Dennis Kozlowski was accused of evading more than $1 million in sales taxes on purchases of artwork ... forcing his resignation as CEO of Tyco, a $38 billion conglomerate. Which led Tyco stock to fall 20 percent overnight, effectively wiping out $5.4 billion of investor value. This being the same Dennis Kozlowski who, in a graduation speech he delivered just three weeks previous, told the graduates of New Hampshire's St. Anselm College that "they would be confronted every day with questions that would test their morals and would force them to think carefully, so as to do the right thing rather than the easy thing."

If Dennis attended Cheryl's graduation, I missed him. I also missed Wayne Taitt's mom, although she was very much present ... albeit miraculously so. That's because last September 11, Wayne's mom was fiddling with her new cell phone, trying to get it to work, which made her late to work ... by five minutes ... for her job at the World Trade Center. Which explains why she was walking through the revolving door on the main floor when the plane hit the building, rather than getting off the elevator on the 85th floor when the plane hit the building. Meaning that not only was she glad to be in Boston for Wayne's graduation, she was glad to be anywhere.

And then there's George Cantor, popular Detroit News columnist. George was at Harvard last week, too. Not because of a kid graduating from Harvard Business School, but because of a kid graduating from Harvard Law School. George's kid took a full class load ... completed it with honors ... co-produced her law school musical ... and became engaged to a young man named Mike ... which would seem to be the stuff of which fairy tales are made (that is, if you factor out the thyroid cancer she contracted last fall). This being the same George Cantor whose other daughter fell to her death through an open window at the University of Michigan a few years previous. Concerning Jaime Cantor's cancer, George (who writes both candidly and movingly about everything) said: "I didn't write about it until now because, what with everything else that has happened to my family, it kind of reduces our lives to a Country Western song."

Five years ago, I wouldn't have compared anybody's life to a Country Western song. But I would have compared it to a board game. In fact, I did. This one, to be exact. It's called Chutes and Ladders. I played it as a kid. But I've lived it as an adult. On one side of the box, it's labeled "age appropriate for 4-to-8-year-olds." Which applies to the playing of it. As concerns the living of it, you have to be at least 50 to understand it.

Last year, at some northern Michigan antique show (which was probably a dressed-up version of a flea market, or maybe a barn sale), Kris bought me a very old version of the game. But I left it up in Elk Rapids and didn't feel I could justify a day just to go retrieve it. In the antique version, there are still ladders. But there are no chutes. Instead, there are snakes (as in "snakes and ladders"). Which may be more biblical. But we'll save that for another time.

For those of you who can't bring yourselves to believe that some of us once played games without benefit of batteries or computers, perhaps a review is in order. The Chutes and Ladders game board has 100 squares, numbered from the bottom to the top of the board. After throwing the dice, each player is permitted to advance by the number of squares indicated on the dice face. The goal, of course, is to reach the 100th square, thereby winning the game.

The twist consists in the fact that certain squares are marked by ladders ... others by chutes. Ladders can propel you ahead of your competition. Chutes can drop you behind. You can be trailing miserably with no hope of winning. Then you hit a tall ladder that catapults you into the lead. Or just the opposite can happen. You can open a terrific lead, finding yourself 20 squares ahead of everyone else. There you sit on square 81. Only 19 squares to go. Then you roll a pair of threes. You move six squares. You land on square 87. Horrors! Square 87 is the launching pad for the longest, nastiest chute on the board. When you are done sliding, you are all the way back at square 24.

The problem with the game is that there is no law governing timing. You know that there are ladders out there. But you don't know when one will be there for you. Ditto for the chutes. You can ride up the ladder, one play … and back down the chute, the next. Or you can play a game where you land on nothing but ladders. Just as you can play a game where you slide down nothing but chutes.

But life's like that. I've seen households where the whole family got on a roll and piled up one victory after another. Everything they touched turned to gold. But I've also seen families where the whole lot of them would have been better off staying in bed for an entire year, given that everything they touched turned to … well, something less than gold.

Is it fair that some should get everything … some shouldn't get anything … and that a few (like the Kozlowskis) should have the wind fill their sails one day, only to have it kicked out of them the next? Of course, it's not fair. But when was life ever fair?

Little kids don't know this. Which is why little kids run around pointing out (usually quite loudly) every violation they spot against life's rule of fairness. They live under the illusion that life is an apple pie which will always be equitably divisible. Then one day they learn that the only rule governing fairness is that there is no rule governing fairness ... and that whatever business God is in, it is not the business of equitably distributing blessings and burdens (so that no one is treated unfairly).

If I have heard it once in my ministry, I have heard it 550 times: "Bill, I have had more than my share." Now I have to tell you that on 549 of those occasions, those individuals were talking about burdens, not blessings. Only once (well, maybe twice) did someone tell me that they had had more than their share of blessings. But whether they had more or less of anything, whatever led them to think ... whatever leads any of us to think ... that burdens and blessings are parceled out as "shares," and that sooner or later (if we just endure long and complain little) everything is going to even out for everybody? Maybe it will. But there's no law that ensures it.

Sometimes chutes and ladders come remarkably close together. I recall a friend standing in my office, resplendent in his tuxedo, thrilled to be awaiting the wedding of his firstborn son. His wife, equally thrilled, is affixing a boutonniere to his lapel. Suddenly, a cell phone rings in his jacket pocket. It is not for me. It is for him. I listen as he hears the news that his father is dead ... of a heart attack ... not totally unexpected ... but terribly timed.

Yet, it can work the other way. I know a young divorcee ... two kids ... old house ... older car ... old dog that gets sick on the rug, five mornings out of seven. She is driving home from work during rush hour. Rain is falling. She is trying to make it to KinderCare before the late charge kicks in. One more late charge and they might refuse to keep her kids any longer. Suddenly she is rear-ended on the roadway. A quick survey of the damage gives her reason to expect that the adjuster will take one look and write the word "totaled." But it is not the adjuster who approaches her. It is the other driver. And rather than writing the word "totaled," he writes his phone number. But she doesn't need to call him. Because he calls her. Later that night. To ask her out. For coffee. And courtship. I marry them a year or so later.

How do I explain that? I don't. And neither do you. In terms of theology, I am probably speaking to ten closet Calvinists this morning who believe that God's hand is behind everything that happens (meaning that, for them, everything is willed). And those ten are balanced by a second ten who believe that God's hand has no causative connection with anything that happens (meaning that, for them, everything is random). Meanwhile, the rest of us look at life and see some things as being providential ... other things as being accidental

… and then spend the rest of our religious lives trying to discern which is which, and what it means.

That's what people of faith do. They try to figure it out in the midst of living it out. And if you are going to find any peace in life (or take any joy from life), you are going to have to put it together in fragments. That's because you are unlikely to get 24 smooth hours in a row. But the wonderful thing is that the Bible understands that. For the Bible was not written by some relaxed scholar in Hawaii, lathered up with sunscreen, sitting under a beach umbrella, drinking lemonade. Rather, the Bible was written by people who had to put their lives together … and put their faith together … out of short pieces of string. Some of the pieces, frayed. Some of them, smooth. Many of them, tangled. A few of them, knotted. All of them, short.

The older I get, the more frequently I revise my list of favorite biblical texts. Of late, it has become clear to me that I must make room for the observation of Ecclesiastes, when the author (whoever he is) writes: "Again I say that the race is not always to the swift … nor the battle to the strong … nor bread to the wise … nor riches to the intelligent … nor favor to the skillful. Rather, time and chance happen to them all."

So, how does the writer suggest we deal with such uncertainties? Well, says Ecclesiastes: "Eat your bread in gladness. Drink your wine in joy." Savor whatever sweetness life may produce. Seize the moment.

Hold fast to it … to the God who is in it … and to the memories that flow from it. Don't overlook or postpone it. For the sweetness you taste today will prepare you for the bitters you may drink tomorrow.

All of which came to mind when, concerning Harvard, his daughter and her cancer, George Cantor wrote: "The night of graduation we took Jaime and Mike out to a great dinner. We laughed a lot, told stories and drank to life." Which sounds like Ecclesiastes (who was a Jew) as told by George (also a Jew). But we three (Kris, Julie and myself) did exactly the same thing … same night … same town … same occasion … and I am not a Jew. Which proves nothing, save for the fact that I am decently grounded in the scriptures and that (in more ways than we realize) biblical faith transcends any number of boundaries.

But textually, I press on. Trampolining through the New Testament, I land first on 2 Timothy who literally shouts: "Persevere. Hang in there. Ride it out. Run the race. Fight the good fight. Finish the course. Keep on, keeping on." That's good advice.

To which the writer of Hebrews adds: "Yes, by all means, persevere. But don't sweat the outcomes. Life is not measured by outcomes. Besides, winning and losing need to be measured on a bigger board than a mere hundred squares. The faithful have never been made perfect in this life. In the short run, nobody wins. Neither does anybody receive everything that was promised." That's good advice.

Jesus seemed to say: "Look, ladders are going to pop up in the most unlikely places … for the most unlikely people … at the most unlikely times. Such ladders are called 'grace.' My father is going to place them wherever He wants. Don't try to figure it out. Don't begrudge my father's generosity. And don't look a gift ladder in the mouth." That's good advice.

But Jesus also seemed to say: "The closer you get to me, the more likely the possibility that you will go down the chute with me. That's what the cross means. But did you ever think that maybe that's how you win? By going down the chute with me?" That's good advice.

And then there are several friends who say the only way you can survive this crazy game board of chutes and ladders, valleys and mountains, downs and ups, is to "cling very close to each other, tonight" … holding on for dear life … to dear life … rejoicing with those who rejoice … weeping with those who weep. That's good advice.

But I somehow keep coming back to Paul and these beautiful words that he tacks onto the end of his letter to the Philippians. He likes the people of Philippi. They have responded to his needs. They have given him money. He is thanking them. Then he adds that he is not merely talking about the money. "For I have learned in whatsoever state I find myself to be content. I know how to be poor. I know how to be rich. I know how to live when the pantry is full. And I know how to live on those days when I go to the refrigerator and there is nothing there but a half-eaten jar of pickles and some seven-week-old cheese. There is no life situation I cannot rise above, given the strength I find in Christ." Only then does he add: "By the way, I did appreciate the money."

Don't get me wrong.

• Paul is not saying: "Whatever happens, happens."

• Paul is not saying: "I have no preference in whatever each day brings."

• Neither is Paul saying: "Chutes and ladders, what do I care? They're all the same to me."

No, Paul cares passionately. As do I. As do you. Which is why I think Paul is saying: "You know, if you open yourself to the possibility that life's roller coaster is a two-seater ... meaning that you do not ride it alone ... you'll make it. You'll make it."

Kris and I have rolls of pictures of graduation week at Harvard. But one of them is priceless. Ask Julie, and she'll show it to you in the narthex. It was taken on that wet and wild Thursday morning. Graduation is history. Julie's cap and gown are history. My suit is history. Kris' dress is history. Three heads of carefully combed hair are history. Looking like drowned rats, dodging puddles of pond-like proportions, we take temporary refuge in a hole-in-the-wall pizza place in Cambridge. The guy who tosses the pizzas recognizes our attire and suggests posing for a picture with Julie. So she goes behind the counter, Kris gets out the camera, and the rest (as they say) is history. Following which we scarf down three slices of Sicilian, chasing them with a trio of Cokes.

Which, as moments go, was as special as they come ... as sweet as they come ... and maybe (for those with eyes to see) as sacramental as they come.

First United Methodist Church
Birmingham, Michigan
June 16, 2002

11

Family Secrets

Scripture: Psalm 139:1-12, I John 4:16b-18

Secrets. Every family has them, keeps them, and pays a greater or lesser price for hiding them. Little did I know the uncharted territory I was entering when I wrote and spoke these words.

Sometime during the evening of Thursday, January 20, after the last program of a busy church had ended and the last member of that busy church had left, the church's pastor ... the only pastor the church had ever known ... the pastor who had started it from scratch and nurtured it from a handful of visitors to over 800 members ... the pastor who, in ten crazy, wonderful and relentlessly-forward-surging years, had led those members from the auditorium of an elementary school to a beautiful facility known as Christ United Methodist Church, Chapel Hill, North Carolina ... the pastor whose vision had led the way and whose energy had carried the day ... locked his church's doors, killed his church's lights and, after barricading himself in his office, turned out his own lights, too (effectively giving death the final round in his twelve-year battle with depression).

His name was Raegan May. And when they talked about "rising suns" in the orbit of North Carolina Methodism, his was the one that loomed largest and shone brightest. Until the eclipse, that is, which left classmates, colleagues, members, and friends, along with his wife, Lee, and his daughters, Emily, Megan and Abbie … trying to make sense of the darkness.

I happened on the scene … well, more to the point, I ventured into the territory … six days after they found him, but only three days after they buried him. Not that I knew him. But the ink was barely dry on his death certificate when my friends at Duke Divinity School told me about him.

Which was a good forewarning to have received on a Thursday prior to entering a Chapel Hill hair salon. Because Kris said I absolutely had to have my few remaining hairs cut and trimmed if I was going to preach in Wilmington the forthcoming Sunday. Not that I regularly go to salons where one pays twice as much to a stylist (whatever happened to the word "barber"?) who takes twice as long. But when your wife says, "Do it," you do it.

As stylists go, she was friendly … although she did cut my ear (because that's what Tar Heels do to Blue Devils). And in the conversation that followed the mop-up, she managed to put enough bits and pieces together so as to figure out what I did for a living. Which prompted some confessing about years of backsliding, even though her mother and daddy (why is it that Southern women always say "daddy" but never say "mommy"?) had taken great pains to turn her into an upstanding Southern Baptist. As if there were any other kind. Then she asked me if I had heard about the suicide of Raegan May ... whose name she didn't know, but whose story she did (hey, Chapel Hill is not that big a place and this was, after all, a beauty shop).

When I told her I had heard about Raegan and "wasn't it a shock and a shame," she said: "Well, you being a preacher and all, is it all right if I ask you a question?" At which point I had no choice. What was I going to say: "No, it isn't all right"? Besides, she had already sliced me once. So she asked her question. And, as she did so, I could see the heads of the adjacent stylists tilt, ever so perceptibly, so as not to miss what I might offer as an answer.

"So is it true what they say (she said), that he will go straight to hell with no possibility of redemption?" Well, you know what I answered. Of course, you know what I answered. Which sufficed. And satisfied. But I did not tell her that my answer was fired in the crucible of firsthand experience. Meaning that I did not tell her about Bill and his choice. Nor did I tell her about eleven years of living with it (never to be confused with "getting over it"). Nor did I tell her I had written a book about it.

People to whom I have told this story seem surprised at my silence. "You are so open," they say, "so honest ... so public ... so unguarded ... so self-revelatory." Which is true. I am. But even I pick my moments. And this was not one of them. I figure there are times to let the shirttail of my soul hang out and times to keep the shirttail of my soul tucked in.

One of you said I should send her a copy of my book. Which I am still pondering. And may still do. But I wonder if she will even remember the conversation ... the question ... let alone me (or my bloody ear). Not that my book didn't surface elsewhere in Chapel Hill at the time of Raegan's death. Truth be told, it surfaced in the sermon at his service. The Dean of Duke Divinity School gave my book to the preacher. Which he borrowed ... rather liberally, as it turned out. But hopefully, helpfully.

Others have found it so. Or so they have said. All but one of the sermons in it, I never planned to preach. Nor, as a collection, did I ever plan to publish. And I wouldn't have published, had not Rod Quainton given them to John Claypool, and had not John Claypool given them to Debra Farrington, and had not Debra's people at Morehouse Publishing come circling back to me. Like I said, I am open and honest. But in my own way, on my own terms. Pulpit appearances to the contrary, I am a rather private person ... one who does not believe that every box should be opened, every closet vacated, and every rock lifted for purposes of show and tell. Making me more like you than you think I am like you.

But the story seemed worth telling. And the sermons seemed worth sharing. And while time does not remove all scars, time does relieve most wounds. So I wrote it all down. Morehouse printed it all up. And when the book saw the light of day last October, several boxes appeared here on the afternoon of Julie and Jared's wedding rehearsal. Which Tina Grubb and Janet Smylie locked away for the weekend (in a gesture of great caring and kindness). Since then the book has gone through several printings. And given its birthplace in an Episcopal publishing house tucked away in Harrisburg, Pennsylvania, has done amazingly well. A trio of newspaper articles helped locally. And thanks to the amazing tentacles of the internet, I have been able to track sales and receive responses nationally.

For it is the responses rather than the sales that interest me, given that the responses are filled with stories. And what is strange is how privately the stories have been held and how closely they have been guarded. Even here at First Church where I thought I knew a lot, I really knew very little. Either because I never asked, or because you never said.

As you will remember, upon purchasing the book you had the option of leaving it for a signature, an inscription, or a short message. For which many of you asked. Not because you wanted my name, but because you wanted me to direct it to someone else's name. Or, in many cases, you wanted me to recall someone else's name ... someone who used to be but is no more.

You expected me to write something personal … something helpful … to someone experiencing something hurtful. Your request came in words written on one page, suggesting words I might write on another page, the better to introduce words printed in a slew of pages, about things for which it is sometimes said: "There are no words." Over and over again I read lines like:

- I never said anything to anyone about this before.

- In our family, this is something nobody wants to talk about.

- I have never known what to say to my mother (father, sister, brother, uncle, cousin, even my best friend). But maybe if I give them your book (with their name written in your hand), it will open a door which has been closed far too long and far too tightly.

A friend of my daughter's in San Francisco took Julie to dinner, introduced the subject of the book, and then asked Julie's opinion about whether she should send it to her father. Apparently, her father's father (meaning her grandfather) committed suicide years and years ago. But nobody ever owned up to how he died, meaning that nobody ever dealt with why he died, or how various members of the family felt about his dying. And because they avoided the subject of his dying, it eventually became easier to avoid the subject of his living, too. Which meant that, over time, it became as if he'd never been. I mean, if you can't talk about "it," you can't talk about him. Because talking about him might introduce the subject of "it."

What she wanted to know was what Julie thought would happen if she were to send my book to her father, accompanied by a note saying: "I think I know what happened to Grandpa. Yet you and I have never talked about what happened to Grandpa. I wonder if maybe we might now ... and whether this book might help us?"

But what she was really asking Julie was: "Have you and your father been able to talk about your brother? How you felt. How your father felt. What was said. What wasn't said." It wasn't permission she was seeking from Julie, or even encouragement she was seeking from Julie, so much as testimony. That's what she was seeking from Julie.

The girl asking the question is in her mid-twenties. Meaning that her father must be in the neighborhood of his mid-fifties. Meaning that the window of opportunity will never be more open. She, being well beyond adolescence. He, being well short of Alzheimer's. But it is entirely possible that if she raises it, he will deny it ... decline to discuss it ... or find ways to avoid it. Why? Because it happens all the time in families.

Families are full of secrets. There are birth secrets (dealing with the when, where, how and who of conception). And there are death secrets (leading to equal, or even greater, layers of deception). Along with behavior secrets (involving things that clearly happened, but which the involved parties were instructed to "keep under your hat" and "never tell a soul").

I used to enjoy going places and doing things with my father. They didn't have to be grandiose or expensive things. Which they never were. Going to see a sandlot baseball game was a good thing. But it was not uncommon for my father to stop on the way home at some watering hole or another and suggest I wait in the car for fifteen minutes or so. "I'll leave the key in the ignition so you can listen to the radio," he would say. And he would return, as promised, in fifteen minutes. But after starting the engine, he would reach over, put his hand on my knee and say: "Don't tell your mother that we stopped. We'll just let this be our little secret." And the first few times it happened, I suppose I felt honored to be trusted. But after that, I felt burdened by being conscripted (into his conspiracy of silence). The truth was, I didn't mind the fifteen minutes. But I hated being linked to the deception that, over time, all but fractured our family.

One of my heroes, Frederick Buechner, writes:

> *"I have come to believe that, by and large, the human family all has the same secrets. Which are both very telling and very important to tell. Telling, in the sense that they reveal the central paradox of our condition ... that what we hunger for (more than anything else) is to be fully known, and yet that is often what we fear more than anything else (being fully known).*
>
> *Yet they are important to tell because otherwise we run the risk of losing track of who we are. And we come to*

accept, instead, the highly-edited version we show the world, in hopes that the world will find the edited version more acceptable than the real thing."2

Go back to the girl in San Francisco who wants to break through years of silence with her father about the death of her grandfather. It has gone on for so long (the silence, I mean) that I am not sure who is being protected. But the casualty is not truth, but love. Because secrets separate. By definition, that's what secrets are designed to do. They keep people apart, by ruling certain subjects "off limits." It is no longer about how grandpa left the world, but about how father and daughter will live together in the world.

Sure, it is risky to upset the status quo. Frightening, too. But the last time I looked, love casts out fear.

- Where there's only a little love, there's a lot of fear.
- Where there's a little more love, there's a little less fear.
- Where there's a lot of love, one finds very little fear.
- And when love becomes perfect, there's a total absence of fear.

The problem being that all human love is imperfect. Which means there will always be some fear. God's love, alone, being perfect. Which is a good thing, given that I read (and we prayed) this morning that "there are no secrets from Him." One of the first prayers I memorized, after I got through "Now I lay me down to sleep," "Our Father," and "Hail Mary, full of grace" (my grandmother being Catholic) was this morning's collect.

Almighty God, unto whom all hearts are open, all desires known, and from whom no secrets are hid ...

No secrets. Can you imagine that? The truth is, you probably can't. The psalmist said (Psalm 139) that such knowledge is too great to grasp. But wonderful, too. For if there is nowhere to hide my deeds ... nowhere to hide my words ... nowhere, even, to hide my thoughts ... then there is nowhere to hide me. The God who searches me and knows me will search me and find me. Anywhere I run. Anywhere I hide.

Heaven?   There.
Sheol?   There.
Light?   There.
Darkness?   There.
Utterly out to sea?   Even There.

And if you read verse 10 carefully, not only will I be sought and found, I will be held and led.

Bringing me full circle to Chapel Hill, North Carolina ... to Raegan

May's suicide … and to the question of my ear-slashing stylist: "So is it true what they say, that he is now damned, doomed and fried, beyond all possibility of redemption?"

To which I said in great theological profundity:

"Hell no."

First United Methodist Church

Birmingham, Michigan

February 27, 2005

Note: This sermon grew out of responses received from my book published in October 2004 entitled Take the Dimness of My Soul Away: Healing After a Loved One's Suicide.

In thinking theologically about unshared stories and closely-held information, I was aided and abetted by rereading Frederick Buechner's volume, Telling Secrets, *where he writes: "I not only have my secrets, I am my secrets. And you are your secrets. Our trusting each other enough to share them has much to do with the secret of what it is to be human."*

As concerns the oft-quoted line, "We are about as sick as the secrets we keep," it sounds like vintage Buechner, but don't hold him hostage to my memory.

And as concerns the stylist in Chapel Hill, I was grateful for her question and her haircut. She provided me with both a good story and a good appearance. Truth be told, I was not really slashed and sliced, so much as nicked. But given the weighty tone of the sermon, the exaggeration of my plight was aimed at providing a lighter touch.

12

Kindly Allow Me to Show You the Door

Scripture: II Corinthians 2:12, Revelation 3:8

For 33 years I was privileged to serve as a trustee of Albion College (a United Methodist institution of higher education). During my tenure, I also served as a lecturer and published a book of college prayers. This sermon was preached at the 2003 Baccalaureate.

Forty-six years ago, my father died in a house that was but four blocks from the house into which he was born. At that point in her life, my mother's journey had covered all of six miles. My people were not traveling people.

Neither were my people college people. My father, who may have been the most well-read man I ever knew, aborted the last half of his senior year in high school by hopping a California-bound freight train with Louie Malchie. And although he probably explained it as "setting off to see the world," what he was actually doing was running away from the world. Which may explain why, years later, he chose to stay home rather than attend my graduation from Yale? I mean, how could he face what I had just finished when it so painfully reminded him of what he had never started.

My mother never went to college either, nor did any of my aunts, uncles or cousins. Meaning that there was no one to chart my way. It was my minister who said, "That boy is going to Albion." So I did. Prior to which, I read no catalogs ... attended no college nights ... visited no campuses ... and received no phone calls from recruiters. Worse yet, I grew up in the dark ages before user-friendly websites and virtual tours. I lived a mere 90 miles from Albion, but nobody ever suggested that we take a Sunday drive to check out the place where I was going to school. The day I unpacked my suitcase in room 331 of Seaton Hall was the first day I ever set eyes on this college. For all I knew, Albion was only one or two exits before the end of the earth.

So how did I get to wherever it is I have gotten to (a terrible sentence, I know, but my choice of words is deliberate)? As part of my answer, I introduce a trio of conversations ... all of them with academicians over a five year period ... at a time when my life could have gone a very different, and far less interesting way.

The first conversation was with Albert Keenan. Mr. Keenan taught literature at Mackenzie High School. And when I took his class in the eleventh grade, I marveled that the Detroit Board of Education would allow someone who was at least eighty-five years old to teach high school students. But they did. Which was amazing.

Ours was a class in English literature. Which was boring. Perhaps because the class occurred at a boring hour … after lunch. And there were days when I wasn't sure if Mr. Keenan wasn't as bored as we were. Which may have been the reason he decided we should read Macbeth … as a class … for several days … out loud. With each of us taking parts as they appeared … and as he assigned.

Well, the time went by, and the pages went by. Eventually, it seemed as if everybody in the class had been called upon to read a part but me. And it wasn't so much that I wanted a part as that I didn't want to be overlooked for a part (which would have felt like being sent to right field after all the better readers had been chosen).

So at the end of a class, I approached him, saying timidly to him: "Mr. Keenan, I have yet to be called upon. So if you need anyone else to read, I'm still unchosen." To which he said: "Be patient, Mr. Ritter. We have bigger things in mind for you." Which turned out to be the meatiest, juiciest role in the play. To this day, I don't remember what he saw in me that led him to assign it to me. Nor do I remember anything else about the class or his role in it. Just that one afternoon when he said "Be patient, Mr. Ritter. We have bigger things in mind for you."

It wasn't long after that I was called down to the principal's office, inhabited by one Joseph Pennock. Who, let the record show, was the only person who ever emerged from the womb with white hair, wearing a three-piece suit. And wouldn't you know that the same Board of Education that allowed an eighty-five-year-old man to teach English literature, also allowed a man ten years his senior to be a principal.

Telling me to sit down opposite him at his desk, he opened a huge book that contained student records ... one page per student. In front of me ... staring at me ... was my record. Every class. Every grade. Decent. But far from stellar. He muttered something about how it could be better. But he allowed as to how that was entirely up to me.

Then he flipped several pages back to the record of Rita Ponte. Which was stellar. I mean, it couldn't have been better. "Take a look at that, Mr. Ritter," he said. And for just a moment ... on that morning ... in that office ... there wasn't anybody in the eleventh grade I hated more than Rita Ponte. After which he said, "Mr. Ritter, sometime during the next year both you and Miss Ponte will be applying to college. With her record, I will be able to do something for her. With your record, there will be far less that I can do for you. But people at this school who know you better than I do, tell me there is no reason her record can't be your record." And from that day forward, it was.

Now advance with me to my senior year here at Albion. I am a pre-ministerial student with a major in philosophy. A new teacher joins the faculty. His name is William Gillham, and he is fresh from Princeton. Bored with the sameness of previous instruction in my field, I take three of his classes in one year. We hit it off. I like him. He likes me. He wants to know where I am going to seminary. I name a pair of schools that are close ... denominationally and geographically. He tells me "No." He tells me I am going inter-denominationally and easterly. He tells me I am going to Yale or Harvard.

I tell him he is nuts. Never have I heard anything so preposterous or impossible. I am certain they will not want me there. Neither can I afford to go there. I even have doubts as to whether I would know what road to take to get there. So I apply and gain acceptance to a pair of seminaries ... nice Methodist seminaries ... in Ohio and Illinois. Where I would have received a decent education. But he refuses to let up. "Just apply out East," he says. "What can it hurt to apply?" So I do. Just to shut him up. I picture the admission committees at Yale and Harvard laughing uproariously as they scan my application before stamping my rejection. But the last laugh was his laugh ... when they did for me what he knew they would do for me. I not only got offers, I got money. And three years later, my take-away from Yale had less to do with better classes taught by better teachers, so much as my astonishing discovery that if I could cut it there, I could probably cut it anywhere ... and maybe I had better open up my eyes a little wider to what God might be asking of me (or getting ready to do with me).

Now my story is not your story. But I have to believe that there have been people here (and maybe even prior to here) who:

- Pushed your buttons

- Scratched your itches

- Widened your horizons

- Triggered your imaginations

- Nudged you … prodded you

- Enchanted you

- Stretched you

- And then showed you the door … and maybe even shoved you through it.

I am talking about people who, while teaching your classes, let you borrow their glasses. So that you could see for yourself what they saw in you … for you … along with what might somehow, some way, someday, be done by you.

And if in that process of assisted self-discovery you said, "Oh, My God," maybe you might want to think about that phrase a little bit. Speaking personally, I'm a little slow. I never seem to know, at any given time, what God is telling me to do … where God is telling me to go … or whose voice God may be using to get my attention. There are other people who claim to know those things … immediately … and with great certainty. Some days I envy them. Other days, I worry about them. I only figure out such things once I've seen them in the rear-view mirror (meaning that to whatever degree there has been a purpose and plan for my life, I "got it" only after I lived it.). Did I recognize their words as being monumental at the time? Of course not. But their words were seed-planting on the way to being life-changing.

And their voices pushed me through the door, which is what I am now doing for you. You get to go tomorrow. But the truth is you gotta go tomorrow. You can't stay here. Even if you'd like to, you can't. Don't take it personally. We like you and all that. But we need your space … your place … your room … your bed … your band uniform … your lab coat … your choir robe … your football jersey. I know it sounds a little cruel. After all, it was just five years ago that we wooed you … pursued you … slobbered and drooled all over you … and even threw major money at you … until you came. And stayed.

Thank you for coming and staying. However, it really is time to go. But let me route you by way of Columbus, Ohio where I once served as a seminary trustee … Methodist Theological Seminary in Ohio … adjacent to Ohio Wesleyan University … on the banks of the Olentangy River. Picture Graduation Saturday in mid-May. See the faculty, students, family members and friends seated on folding chairs in the great, green, grassy quadrangle facing the pillars of the library. Now watch as a scared-stiff student body president steps to the podium, having been chosen to speak a final word on behalf of the graduating seniors. Peering at this assemblage of dignitaries, teachers, classmates, and friends, he runs the gamut of things that nervous speakers do. He plays with his hair. He plays with his tie. He plays with his notes. He plays with the microphone. He sighs ... coughs ... clears his throat ... until he finally says.

The chairs in which we sit are not the chairs of the prophets and the apostles.

The chairs in which we sit are not the chairs at the left hand of power or the right hand of glory.

The chairs in which we sit are not the chairs of the last, or even the next-to-last, judgment.

The chairs in which we sit are the property of the Greater Columbus Ohio Rent-All Society.

Which was true. They were. Rented, I mean. As will be true of your chairs tomorrow. The All Star Rental Company in Jackson will truck them in in the morning and truck them out again at night. By noon tomorrow, the quadrangle will be full of chairs. By sundown, they will all be gone. Albion is a rented chair. But then, life itself is a rented chair. No occupancy is permanent. But from time to time, how good some chairs feel. And how nicely some chairs fit. And to whatever degree your chairs at Albion felt good and fit nice, I hope you are grateful.

So let's wrap this up and put it to bed. Tony Campolo writes:

I was in New York ... now there's a joyless place. I got on an elevator full of dead, joyless people. They were just standing there with attaché cases. And when I got on, I did my thing. I waited for the door to close. You know how people stand and look at the door or the numbers. And as soon as the door closed, I thought I might bring a little joy to the ride. So I turned and smiled at everybody. And in New York, they can't handle that. Which is why they kinda backed away from me.

So I said: "Lighten up, guys. This is a tall building, so we're going to be traveling together for a while. What do you say we sing?" And these suckers were so intimidated by me; they did. I mean, you shoulda been there. They were holding their attaché cases going, "You are my sunshine, my only ..." I got off at the 70th floor, and this guy gets off with me. So I said: "Are you going to the same meeting I'm going to? To which he answered, "No, I just wanted to finish the song."[3]

Members of the class of 2013, while plans are already in place to recycle your space, trust me ... we'll be listening for your singing.

Albion College Baccalaureate Service
Albion, Michigan
May 10, 2013

13

On Dancing a Confirmation Dance

Scripture: Romans 12:1-2

For 25 years of my ministry, I taught the weekly confirmation class of middle schoolers. And for all 40 years, I preached the Confirmation Sermon. I wrote each of these sermons for the confirmands. Delivering it to them. Not to their parents. Not to their siblings. Not to the rest of the congregation. But to them.

Dear Members of the Confirmation Class:

This is your day. This is your hour. And this is your sermon. Everybody else in the room can listen in. But I wrote it for you. Some of you may be wondering about the word "dance" in my sermon title. Don't worry. I'm not going to make you choose partners and move to

167

any music … fast or slow. Because that would surprise all of you … and embarrass more than a few of you.

Besides, I don't know if you even like dancing. When I was in the sixth grade, I didn't. Of course, when I was in the sixth grade, rock and roll wasn't even around. But we had dancing in school. It was a part of our gym class, as I remember it. Some days we played softball. Some days we played dodgeball. Some days we climbed a braided rope from floor to ceiling. And some days we danced. Not that we liked it all that much. But we did it. I remember learning how to square dance in gym class. And I remember learning how to slow dance in gym class.

When we came to the end of the "slow dance unit," we had a big formal dance in the gym. Guys were supposed to clean up, as I remember it. They even suggested we tuck in our shirt … slick down our hair … wear a tie … that kind of thing. Then we were supposed to demonstrate everything we'd learned about dances like the waltz and the foxtrot. We danced to records … 78 rpm records … which went round and round on turntables … and were activated by needles. Like I said, it was a long time ago … shortly after the dinosaurs left.

And we couldn't dance every dance with the same partner. We had a dance card. And we had to have it all filled out before we got to the gym. If there were ten dances, I had to have ten different girls' names on my card. Every time the music stopped, I had to go find the next girl. It wasn't all that much fun. As I remember it, I liked dodgeball better; at least when I was in the sixth grade.

So why is the word "dance" in a sermon title about Confirmation? One reason. Because Confirmation, like dancing, is something you do with your feet. To be sure, other parts of your body are involved ... and, hopefully, your heart. But in a few minutes, we're going to ask you to get on your feet. Then we're going to ask you to come up front. And, surprise of surprises, we're not going to ask your parents to come with you.

Every other time something big has happened in your life ... like when you joined the Brownies ... or when you won the spelling bee ... or when you earned a merit badge or two ... somebody from your family came up and stood behind you. More often than not, somebody even stuck a pin on your mother. But your mother isn't going to follow you today. Neither is your dad. Not that they don't care. But when you come up to the front, you're going to come by yourself. They're going to stand in their pew when we call your name. But they're not going to move. This time, you're on your own.

Years ago, they said they would make sure you were a part of the church. Years ago, they said they would try to introduce you to Jesus Christ. And, for better or worse, they did that job. But this is your time. They can't go on doing everything for you. You need to stand up for yourself. And you need to step out on your own. You can't live on your parents' faith forever.

Which makes your parents proud. But which also makes your parents nervous. Parents always get nervous when kids begin to do things "on their own." Because once you're old enough to cross a few streets ... or make a few decisions ... your parents aren't quite sure where you are going to go, or what you are going to do. They are especially worried about who you are going to follow. Parents are people who were taught ... most likely in prenatal classes ... to say things like: "I don't care what everyone else is doing ... you are not everyone else." My father always took that one step further by saying: "If everybody else got in line and jumped off a cliff, would you jump off the cliff, too?" I never told him I thought his question was ridiculous. But what was equally ridiculous was the fact that, if the cliff wasn't too high, I might have said "yes."

But my father had a point. I was different ... and he was just trying to help me remember that. But, I also had a need to belong ... and he was trying to force me to state my own terms of belonging.

A friend of mine, also named William, presently preaches at Duke University. It is a big and important position. But when he was growing up in South Carolina, he was anything but big and important. And he, too, was concerned about blending in with the other kids. But his mother was equally concerned that he not bend too far in order to blend too much ... especially when he became a teenager ... especially when he began to date ... especially when he began to drive the car. And so it was that whenever he walked out the door (front door ...

back door ... porch door ... garage door), the last thing she would say to him was: "William, remember who you are."

But what did that mean? It's not like he was going to forget his name. Besides, if his mom was like my mom, his name was stitched in his underwear. And it wasn't like she was saying: "Don't forget your keys ... don't forget your manners ... don't forget your billfold." In fact, it wasn't even like she was saying: "Don't forget to put gas in the car ... don't forget to be home by 11:00." It was more than that. She was saying: "Don't forget who you are ... don't forget who your family is." Or (as they say in the south), "Don't forget who your people are. Don't forget who you belong to or what you believe in." I imagine that (on more than one occasion) he wished she'd forget to remind him to remember, so that (for one night) he could go out and forget who he was. Which was probably why she never forgot to remind him to remember.

Every time you walk out the door, you carry a family name ... a family history ... a family hope ... and a whole laundry list of family values. Whether you understand all that or not ... whether you like all that or not ... whether you plan to honor all that or not (once you get out on your own) ... that is who you are. It's in your bones. It's in your genes. It's in that computer in your head that you call a memory. And it's also in your heart. "Who you are," is like underwear you never take off. Even if you get 500 miles from home and never have to walk out your front door again, you will never be able to shake that voice telling you: "Remember who you are."

And you know what? From this morning on, you have something else to remember. You have to remember that you are a disciple of Jesus Christ. A few minutes from now, Matt and I are going to put our hands on your head ... crack through 17 layers of hair spray ... call your name out loud and say: "Andy, the Lord defend you with his heavenly grace, and by his Spirit confirm you in the faith and fellowship of all true disciples of Jesus Christ." Which means that you belong to Jesus. And which is going to make you different from people who don't belong to Jesus. You are never going to be able to wear the uniform of the world without realizing that underneath it (in addition to your underwear) you also wear your relationship with Jesus Christ. Which means that there will be times when you will not fit in with other crowds ... when you will look different ... unusual ... odd (or weird). Or to recall Paul's language:

> *Do not model your behavior on the contemporary world,*
> *but let the renewing of your minds transform you, so*
> *that you may discern for yourselves what is the will of*
> *God ... what is good and acceptable and mature.*

And I suppose you are wondering (along about now): "Just how odd is that going to make me?" Well, in your grandparents' day, kids who followed Jesus Christ were expected to be pretty darned different. They didn't play cards. They didn't go to movies. They didn't go dancing. They didn't wear makeup. And they especially didn't do those things on Sunday.

Fortunately, those days were pretty much over by the time I came along. I danced. I went to movies. I played cards. And the fact that I chose not to wear makeup had nothing to do with Jesus Christ. To this day, I have a profound respect for groups that practice their faith by limiting their contacts with things that others call "worldly." But I am not suggesting that (as soon as you are confirmed) you go home, scrub your face, burn all your CDs and never dance another beat again.

What I am suggesting is that ... at every critical turn in your life ... you ask yourself: "Does the fact that I am a follower of Jesus Christ have anything to say to me here?" If you do that, I think a couple of good things are likely to happen.

First, you will occasionally find yourself doing some "lowly" work. You will remember that, on the night before he died, Jesus washed the disciples' feet. Which was lowly work. Dirty work. Smelly work. But as he went from friend to friend with basin and towel, he said: "Love does things like this." Which it does. Love sometimes stoops down in order to do the simplest things for the neediest people. A nurse gives up a month's vacation to change bandages in a mission hospital. A visitor to the hospital, overcome by the ugliness and smell of it all, blurts out without thinking: "I wouldn't do that for a million dollars." "Neither would I," answers the nurse. "Neither would I."

If you follow Jesus Christ, you will never again be able to look at somebody else's need and say: "I don't care. It's not my problem. No sweat off my back." To be a follower of Jesus Christ means looking out for people. It also means looking to find Jesus in the presence of other people.

Gert Behenna was a rough, big-boned woman who was very much an alcoholic. Sometime after her 50th birthday, she met Jesus Christ, gave up the booze, put her life together, and began telling her story. She became a celebrity on the Christian speaking circuit. But since she didn't like to fly, she drove from place to place. Which meant that she spent a lot of time in her car. And which also meant that she spent a lot of time in gas station restrooms ... which, she said, were so gross that she felt like wearing boots every time she entered one. It got so bad that she complained to the Lord about the terrible inconvenience that was associated with driving around the country speaking for him.

Then, one day, it was as if she heard Jesus saying to her: "Gert, whatever you do for the least of my people, you do for me." And then she said: "Lord, do you mean you use these restrooms, too?" Which was when she realized that Jesus Christ might be the next person coming in after her. So she figured she had better stop complaining and do something. She writes: "Now, when I go into a messy restroom, I pick up all the towels and stuff them into the wastebasket. Then I take another paper towel and wipe off the sink, the mirror, and the toilet seat. After leaving it as clean as possible, I say: 'Here it is Lord, I hope you enjoy it.'"

Don't miss the point, kids. The point is not that you ought to go home and clean the bathrooms (although I could probably get your mothers to give good money to leave the matter just as it stands). The point is that followers of Jesus Christ are going to find him ... and serve him ... in some of the world's messier places, while looking after some of the world's messiest people. It's not always pretty. But once you're a Christian, you can't turn your back.

Second, in addition to doing some lowly work, Jesus Christ is going to ask you to make some hard choices. Six months after I was confirmed ... in the winter of my seventh-grade year ... something incredibly significant took place in my life. My neighborhood was about to change with the movement of a single black lady and her two children into a house on Northlawn Avenue (four blocks away). Everybody was afraid of the change. And everybody was angry, which is often what happens when people become afraid. This poor lady (and her two little kids) were harmless. But she was the first black person coming into our neighborhood. So for three nights running, people gathered in the street by her house ... more or less milling around ... and, I suppose, making her life miserable. And on the day before the second night, several of my friends said: "Let's go over to Northlawn and throw rocks at the black lady's house." The idea of being with my friends sounded cool. And the idea of being part of the action sounded exciting. But, somehow, I knew that I couldn't throw rocks at the "black lady's house." And, what's more, I knew that I couldn't go on thinking of her as "the black lady." So I didn't go.

And I wish I could tell you that I was able to stand up and tell my friends that Jesus Christ was the reason I couldn't. But I couldn't tell my friends that. Not just then. A couple of years later, I could have told my friends that. But, at the time, I just made up some excuse about too much homework (or said that my mother wouldn't let me out of the house). But, in my heart, I knew that the reason I couldn't go had something to do with my Confirmation ... what I had said there ... and who I had said "yes" to there. So, Andy ... Ana ... James ... Brooke ... Taylor ... Colin ... Matthew ... Graham ... Kevin ... Todd ... Sarah ... Erich ... Meghan ... Royce ... Chad ... Evan ... Liz ... Doug ... Zack ... Lissa ... Sarah ... Hunter ... Garrett ... James ... Jon ... Evan ... Jenni ... Jack ... David ... Laynie ... Jonathan ... Kesey ... Steve ... Richard ... Justin ... Becca ... Casey ... Emily ... Katherine ... Michelle ... Rob...Alex ... Brittany ... Will ... Madison ... Alexander ... at every critical turn in your life, I trust you will ask yourself: "Does the fact that I am a follower of Jesus Christ have anything to say to me here?" Because I think it does. And if it doesn't, I think it should. So when Matt gives you the high sign, dance your way up here. And when you leave the church at the close of the service, remember who you are.

First United Methodist Church
Birmingham, Michigan
June 14, 1998 - 11:00 Service

14

On Singing a Baccalaureate Song

Scripture: Mark 1:16-20

In my final two pastoral appointments, we honored our graduates (at whatever level) on a Sunday early in June. We gave them a gift. They wore their caps and gowns. And I fashioned a sermon specifically for them. When I preached a large portion of it at Albion College for the Opening Convocation, 1500 students and faculty, including the President, actually sang the Eensy Weensy Spider song.

It has occurred to me that most graduation speeches ... including mine ... are not terribly memorable. But I keep trying. As do others.

Over the course of the Memorial Day weekend, I spent four days in Elk Rapids. Late one evening, while channel-surfing in search of some athletic contest, I stumbled across the C-Span network. Somebody was delivering a graduation speech. I could tell by the garb. So I listened awhile. Subsequently, I learned that C-Span was replaying a slew of graduation speeches, one right after the other, over the course of several days. And before the long weekend was over, I must have heard excerpts from twenty such efforts. They were delivered by professors and politicians … poets and philosophers. All of them, solid. All of them, scholarly. But none of them, memorable.

Save for two. The first of which was delivered by a Unitarian preacher and culture commentator named Robert Fulghum. Not everybody knows Fulghum's name, but everybody knows his first book: *All I Really Need to Know, I Learned in Kindergarten*. Actually, Fulghum writes some good stuff. And his titles are fantastic. It's hard to pass up book covers that read *It Was On Fire When I Lay Down on It*, *Uh Oh*, and *Maybe, Maybe Not*. But Fulghum's best book may be his serious attempt to discuss the rituals of our lives in a work entitled *From Beginning to End*.

At any rate, Robert Fulghum was invited to deliver a graduation address at Syracuse University. What would he say? At first, he didn't say anything. He just stood there … dressed in academic regalia … making silly motions with his hands and fingers. But then the motions became recognizable. For there wasn't a person in the audience (including me), who hadn't seen or made them.

Once the initial motions were complete, Fulghum repeated them.

Only this time he burst into song. Whereupon everybody in his audience (including me) began to sing with him. And, to whatever degree the spirit moves you, I invite you to sing with me now.

The eensy-weensy spider climbed up the water spout.

Down came the rain and washed the spider out.

Out came the sun and dried up all the rain.

And the eensy-weensy spider climbed up the spout again.

With apologies to "Jesus Loves Me," "The Eensy-Weensy Spider" is probably the first song we learned as children. But there is more to it than meets the eye. Let's dissect it for a closer look.

The eensy-weensy spider climbed up the water spout.

What do we learn? We learn that a very small-in-stature spider commenced to climb. I suppose it is in the nature of spiders to be small. And also to climb. As to this thing about water spouts, I can't rightly say. I'm not all that "into" spiders. Why a water spout? Because it was there, I suppose.

All things considered, most of you are bigger than spiders. So why have you been climbing like them? Several reasons, I suppose.

- Because the light is better up there.
- Because the view is better up there.

179

- Because the pay is better up there.
- And because things thin out up there ... so you won't feel crowded, trapped and lost in the crowd.

Down came the rain and washed the spider out.

Rains will come ... which won't all be "showers of blessing." And all the Doppler Radar in the world won't alert you to their arrival. But when they come, they will interrupt your "king of the hill" game, big time ... even as they slow your "climb, climb up Sunshine Mountain." Such rains will come in the form of:

- a class you can't pass
- a boss you can't please
- a job you can't do
- a diagnosis you can't dodge
- a biopsy that won't lie
- or a friend who will
- an addiction you can't kick out
- or a lover you can't coax back.

As concerns such rains, the issue is not "if" but "when." The author of Ecclesiastes is right. "Time and chance really do happen to us all."

A tough kid once approached me and said: "Ritter, do you know what a swirly is?" Upon learning that I didn't, he said: "A swirly is when I put your head in the toilet and flush." Fortunately, I talked him out of his intention. But life often accomplishes what he didn't … grabbing our heads and flushing all over us.

Out came the sun and dried up all the rain.

Which means that good things will also happen in your life.

- Fortune will smile on you.
- Friends will smile on you.
- Love will smile on you.
- God will smile on you.

And … as with the adversities … you won't be able to explain the "good stuff," either. "Why me?" is not only something we cry in the rain. "Why me?" is also something we cry in the sun. For most of you have already been kissed by sunshine. I mean, do you think you got this far by your own efforts?

- Because you were all that good?
- Because you were all that gifted?
- Because you were all that gorgeous?
- Because you were all that godly?

Well, if that's what you are thinking, I suggest you cut the self-made ("I did it my way") crap, long enough to acknowledge that you got this far (and did this much) because a whole lot of wonderful people got in your way ... I mean, literally, got in your way. Perhaps, because they were placed in your way. I mean, they didn't all get there by accident, did they? How is it they showed up exactly where you needed them ... and exactly when you needed them? When I take a long view of history, I see my life as having been laced with people who showed up at just the right time, and doors that opened when I didn't have anyplace else to go.

And the eensy-weensy spider climbed up the spout again.

The spider was not easily deterred. Which is why this song is the quintessential American anthem. And which is why there wasn't anybody in the room, a few moments ago, who couldn't remember it ... or wouldn't sing it. In addition to being in our brains, I would contend that the "eensy-weensy spider" is also in our blood.

But I want to push you toward a second song. This one has no motions. Although it does have words. But, before we sing the text, I want to hum the tune. And when it becomes sufficiently familiar so as to permit you to hum along, I invite you to join me.

I see you all know this one, too. We sing it under the title "Joyful, Joyful, We Adore Thee." But it wasn't written with that text in mind ... which is why I had us hum it first. In its own way, it's something of an onward-and-upward song, composed by an onward-and-upward man (who, in his earthly life, got rained on plenty).

I'm talking about Ludwig van Beethoven. Born in 1770, he was raised in the home of a poor musician (are there any other kind?). More to the point, his father was described by one biographer as a "drunken tenor." Beethoven was gifted but troubled. Something of a loner, he was multiply disappointed in love. Given to unseemly behavior and deplorable manners, he often played practical jokes which backfired, depriving him of the camaraderie he craved. He accepted responsibility for a nephew who brought him great disappointment. At age 30 he began to experience a hearing loss. By age 49 he was totally deaf. And for the last eight years of his life, he couldn't carry on an audible conversation. A portrait of Beethoven at his piano, painted during his deaf period, depicts the piano as something of a wreck. Apparently, he pounded it into submission in an effort to play it loud enough to hear the notes.

Yet, four years before he died, he composed his ninth (and final) symphony, closing with the memorable melody we now refer to as the "Ode to Joy." Soaring and passionate, it almost begs for a religious interpretation. And while Beethoven was not institutionally religious, he once penned in a journal: "Every tree seems to say holy, holy."

In 1911, a Presbyterian Princetonian named Henry Van Dyke wrote lyrics to it, fleshing out its religious potential. *Moments ago, we sang Van Dyke's lyric:*

Joyful, joyful, we adore thee,

God of glory, Lord of love.

Hearts unfold like flowers before thee,

Opening to the sun above.

Melt the clouds of sin and sadness,

Drive the dark of doubt away.

Giver of immortal gladness,

Fill us with the light of day.

Ah, the beginnings of an answer. It is God who causes the spirit to soar. It is God who responds to the rains ... without and within. And it is God who inspires (and rewards) the upward climb. Consider Van Dyke's fourth verse:

Mortals, join the mighty chorus (meaning, we are not alone)

Which the morning stars began. (even nature joins in)

Love divine is reigning o'er us,

Binding all within its span.

And here comes the good part.

Ever singing, march we onward,

Victors in the midst of strife.

Joyful music leads us sunward,

In the triumph song of life.

What do we have here? What we have is the "eensy-weensy spider" all dressed up for church. What we have is a reminder that this "upward climb" is both God-inspired and well-nigh universal. People have done it before us. People will do it after us. We encourage it from generation to generation. Thirty-six years ago, at an Albion College baccalaureate, I heard Henry Hitt Crane say:

> A tired old doctor died one day,
> And a baby boy was born.
> A little new soul all pink and frail,
> And a soul that was tired and worn.
> And halfway here and halfway there,
> On a high white cloud of shining air,
> They met ... and passed ... then paused to speak
> In the flushed and hearty dawn.
>
> And the man looked down at the bright new child
> With wise and wearied eyes.
> While the little chap stared back at him
> In startled, scared surmise.
> And then he shook his downy head.
> "I think I'll not be born," he said,
> "For you look old ... and tired ... and gray ..."
> As he shrank from the pathway of the skies.
>
> But the tired old doctor roused once more
> At the battle cry of birth.

And there was memory in his eyes

Of pain … and toil … and mirth.

"Go on," he said,

"It's good … it's bad … it's hard … it's ours, my lad."

And he stood and waved him out of sight

On to the waiting earth.4

•••••••

I suppose I could stop here. And I probably should stop here. But I want to say one more thing, even as I introduce one more song. Sticking with this idea of "the upward climb," let me ask: "Might your climb be undertaken in response to a call? And might that call originate outside you, rather than inside you?"

At the beginning of this little exercise, I told you I remembered a pair of speeches that I saw on C-Span. The second was offered by a trumpeter. The man's name was Wynton Marsalis. His audience was Haverford College. He came to the podium holding a trumpet. But before he put his lips to the mouthpiece, he talked about his middle school band teacher. He described the first day of the semester when the teacher passed out instruments to various members of the class. To a skinny kid with thick glasses, the teacher gave a clarinet. To a fat kid with big lips, the teacher gave a tuba. "Then," said Wynton Marsalis, "for reasons I can't begin to fathom, he handed a trumpet to me. Then he told us to play. We were terrible. Anybody would have said we were terrible. But he told us we were good. Apparently, he could see something in us that we couldn't see in ourselves. And that was the day I was called to play the trumpet."

Bill's "Faith Friends," Jamie Hinz and Mallory Hinz at Southern Methodist University's 2016 Commencement

Could God have a call for you? Could God see something in you that you aren't able to see in yourself? And might God be calling you to a work you never considered (like this work) … in a place you never considered working (like a church)? In a moment, we will sing:

> *Lord, you have come to the lakeshore,*
>
> *Looking neither for wealthy nor wise ones.*
>
> *You only ask me to follow humbly.*

> *O Lord, with your eyes you have searched me,*
>
> *And while smiling, have spoken my name.*
>
> *Now my boat's left on the shoreline behind me.*
>
> *By your side, I will seek other seas.*

Could this year be that lakeshore? And could the "smiling Lord" be speaking your name?

I worry about the ministry. Not because God has stopped calling people … but because some of us are not doing enough to amplify that call so that people like yourselves no longer turn deaf ears to it.

Rest assured, God will never call you to something you are unequipped to do. And God will never call you to something the world doesn't desperately need to have done. But if you're waiting to be struck by lightning or hit by a holy hammer, you could wait all night. Because it probably won't happen that way.

God never inserted himself into one of my dreams or pounded my stubborn will into submission during a period of heavy prayer. Like I said earlier, God "got in my way" … with some of the most unlikely people you could ever imagine. There were a couple of young preachers who never said much about the ministry, but portrayed it appealingly. And there were a handful of silver-haired old ladies who, because they couldn't fathom why a teenager would hang around a church as much as I hung around mine, began to say things like: "I bet you're going to be a minister." Little did they know that the reason I hung around church so much was because it provided a well-ordered oasis from some of the turmoil that was going on in my home. And then there was a tired old English Lit teacher who told me the only thing he would remember about the semester was listening to me read Shakespeare.

These were they who called me into ministry. And I've spent the rest of my life trying to figure out if they were right.

But most days, I wake up, knowing that I am:

- where I need to be
- where I want to be
- where I ought to be
- where God can make use of me.

And I have never ... even once ... wondered about the worthwhileness of what I am doing. I see people from the top of the mountain to the bottom of the valley. I see them sad. I see them happy. I see them needy. I see them seedy. I see them screwing up. I see them straightening up. I see them struggling. I see them soaring. I've seen God do some pretty extraordinary things ... to some pretty ordinary people ... through some less-than-ordinary people. And while I have never seen Jesus turn water into wine, I have seen Jesus turn beer into furniture.

And you could, too. Your mother used to say to you: "What in the name of God are you doing?" Well ... what in the name of God are you doing?

First United Methodist Church
Birmingham, Michigan
June 14, 1998 - 9:30AM

15

On Transposing Sheet Music into Sweet Music

Over the course of 40 years, I preached on sex-related themes multiple times. But never quite like this. Several months later, I preached it in the chapel at Duke Divinity School. On that occasion, The Song of Solomon was the lectionary selection for the day, and the chaplain said: "Our community needs to hear this, given the assumption of many of the faculty that divinity students are alive only from the neck up."

Scripture: Song of Solomon   A Tasting Menu

She speaks:

>Let him kiss me with the kisses of his mouth.
>
>For your love is better than wine,
>
>your anointing oils are fragrant,
>
>your name is perfume poured out:
>
>therefore the maidens love you.

Draw me after you,

let us make haste.

With great delight I sat in my beloved's shadow,

and his fruit was sweet to my taste.

He brought me to the banqueting house,

and his intention toward me was love.

Sustain me with raisins,

refresh me with apples;

for I am faint with love.

Oh, that his left hand were under my head,

and his right hand embraced me.

The voice of my beloved.

Look, he comes leaping upon the mountains,

bounding over the hills,

my beloved is like a gazelle, or a young stag.

Look, there he stands behind our wall,

gazing in at the windows, looking through the lattice.

My beloved speaks and says to me:

"Arise, my love, my fair one, and come away;

for now the winter is past,

the rain is over and gone.

The flowers appear on the earth;

the time of singing has come,

and the voice of the turtledove is heard in our land."

(and when Ernie Harwell read these words at the beginning of every spring training, you thought they were about baseball)

Upon my bed at night,

I sought him whom my soul loves;

I sought him, but found him not.

I called him, but he gave no answer.

I will rise now and go about the city.

I will seek him in the streets and in the squares.

I sought him, but found him not.

The sentinels found me as they went about the city.

"Have you seen him whom my soul loves?" I asked.

Scarcely had I passed them when I found him.

I held him and would not let him go.

He speaks:

How beautiful you are, my love,

how very beautiful.

Your eyes are doves behind your veil.

Your hair is like a flock of goats,

moving down the slopes of Gilead.

Your teeth are like a flock of shorn ewes,

that have come up from the washing,

all of which bear twins

and not one among them is bereaved.

Your lips are like a crimson thread

and your mouth is lovely.

Your cheeks are like halves of a

pomegranate behind your veil.

Your neck is like the tower of David.

You are altogether beautiful, my love;

there is no flaw in you.

You have ravished my heart, my bride,

you have ravished my heart with a glance of your eyes,

with one jewel of your necklace.

How much better is your love than wine.

Your lips distill nectar,

Honey and milk are under your tongue.

I eat my honeycomb with my honey,

I drink my wine with my milk,

eat, friends, drink,

and be drunk with love.

How graceful are your feet in sandals, O queenly maiden.

Your rounded thighs are like jewels,

the work of a master hand.

Your flowing locks are like purple;

a king is held captive in the tresses.

She speaks:

I am my beloved's,

and his desire is for me.

Come, my beloved,

let us go forth into the fields and lodge in the villages;

let us go early to the vineyards,

and see whether the vines have budded,

whether the grape blossoms have opened,

and the pomegranates are in bloom.

There I will give you my love.

Set me as a seal upon your heart,

for love is strong as death,

passion fierce as the grave.

Its flashes are flashes of fire, a raging flame.

Many waters cannot quench love,

neither can floods drown it.

If one offered for love all the wealth of his house,

it would be utterly scorned.

Sermon

Her name was Ann. His name was Dean. They were young friends of mine and good friends of each other. Both with good backgrounds. Both with good educations. Both with bright futures. Everybody said so.

But that's not all everybody said. "How right for each other," friends said. Family said it. Preacher (meaning me) said it. Why, it was as plain as the noses on their faces. Having met, they should mingle. And having mingled, they should march ... straight to the altar (so they might mate and make babies together).

But there was one small problem. They couldn't see what everyone else saw. Oh, they liked each other. They kept company with each other. They honored the deeply-held values of each other. Both were involved in the church. Both dabbled a bit in amateur theater. Theirs was a great friendship. But neither wanted to risk the friendship by suggesting anything more. After all, best friends don't come along every day.

But one day ... after about four years of this ... they made an appointment to come and see me. At which time (with incredibly sheepish and silly grins) they asked me to officiate at their wedding. Knowing them as well as I did, I figured that something dramatic must have happened to transpose their relationship into a new key. So I asked what it was. Which was when Ann looked at me, looked at Dean, and then responded: "One day I simply said, 'Enough of this.' And I leaned over and kissed my best friend."

Which, with a nod in the direction of Jimmy Rogers, must have been one of those kisses that was sweeter than wine. I, for one, would never underestimate the life-giving power of a kiss. Or its therapeutic

Wedding of Ann Brown and Dean Moening

value, either. A couple of weeks ago, this book came on the market (newly-published by Abingdon Press) entitled *Reflections on Marriage and Spiritual Growth.* It contains contributions ("essays," you might call them) from 16 couples … including Kris and myself.

In my wife's section, she quotes from a recent German study that reports remarkable benefits to husbands who kiss their wives each morning. Those lucky husbands have fewer auto accidents, are sick less often, live an average of five years longer, and earn 20-30% more money over the course of their career. The study doesn't speak of similar benefits for wives. But while I know relatively little about the study Kris cites, I'll be a more-than-willing participant in any additional research she chooses to do.

I make no apology for starting this sermon with words about kisses. Because that's exactly where the text starts … with words about kisses. I am talking "Song of Solomon" here … sometimes called Song of Songs or (in an earlier era) Canticle of Canticles. When I read portions of it moments ago, you couldn't believe your ears. And I edited some of the lines better suited to a private reading than a public one. A couple of days ago, two of you told me that you read Song of Solomon to each other. Out loud. And something in your telling suggested that I might be embarrassed, were I to do any further inquiring. All I know is that Kevin Leman commends the practice for lovers (reading out loud from the Song of Solomon, I mean).

Yes, I am talking about the same Kevin Leman who was here two weekends ago … the same Kevin Leman who packed the sanctuary on

Sunday night and nearly packed it again on Monday night ... the same Kevin Leman who sold every book he shipped to us in advance (and could have sold 200-300 more, had they been available) ... the same Kevin Leman who talked about things in this sanctuary on Sunday night that I never thought I'd hear discussed in this place (yet not one person has written, even anonymously, to complain) ... and the same Kevin Leman who told you (albeit with tongue in cheek) that I was going to preach a twelve-Sunday sermon series on this same Song of Solomon, read to you earlier.

"What is this book?" you say. Darned if anybody knows, I say. It's been preached as an allegory of God's love for Israel, or Christ's love for the church. Which is okay, I guess. But it's neither. It's been preached as the prose of King Solomon's early period ... with the Book of Proverbs being the prose of King Solomon's middle period, and the Book of Ecclesiastes being the prose of King Solomon's final period. But it's not. And it's been taught in advanced Old Testament courses (we're talking the final year of seminary, now) as liturgical material from the corrupted worship of the Jerusalem Temple (necessitating Josiah's reform in 621 B.C.) ... or as an ancient Tammuz liturgy from the Adonis Cult (itself borrowed from an even more ancient Canaanite fertility ritual) ... or as a set of dramatic poems read during Hebrew wedding festivities.

Simply put, nobody knows. So if we don't know what it was once, the more interesting question becomes: "Why is it in the Bible now?"

Out of all the writings available for Israel to choose ... or available for later Councils to purge ... why was this book kept? Everybody I read agrees on the answer. The Song of Solomon is in the Bible, not because every holy book needs a dose of Danielle Steele to keep the reader awake. Instead, the Song of Solomon is in the Bible because it "sings the praise of the greatest force in the world ... that which builds the universe from atom to man ... draws individuals together in fruitful union ... forms the foundation on which mutual relations can profitably rest ... rears families ... organizes societies ... interprets nature ... lifts shining ideals ... and gives the touch divine to all existence." Mind you, I didn't write that. Nathaniel Schmidt did. But it's lofty prose.

So let's boil it down. We're talking "love" here ... sensuous, passionate, romantic love ... "love that is as hungry as the sea." Biblically speaking, we're talking the kind of longing that is initially encountered in the first two pages of the Bible when the man says: "At last" (as in "finally" ... or as in "God, what took you so long?"). More to the point, the man says: "At last, this is bone of my bone and flesh of my flesh. This one is worth leaving mama and daddy for." Which is the same longing found in the last two pages of the Bible, when the new Jerusalem is depicted how? "As a bride adorned for her husband," that's how. And we're not talking "wedding dress" here. Meaning that we move from images of nakedness ("and they were naked and not ashamed") in Genesis 2:24 to negligee ("prepared as a bride adorned for her husband") in Revelation 21:2.

But in between Genesis 2:24 and Revelation 21:2, the Bible portrays intimacy and passion as being more problematical than promising, having more to do with the language of "guilt" than with the language of "gift." Except, that is, for one spot. I am talking about the Song of Solomon, which is like a rare oasis upon which lovers stumble, just when they think that love is surely doomed, lovers are always hurt, and passion (which blossoms early) loses fragrance quickly. To which the Song of Solomon says: "Oh no. You've got it wrong. Look again. It's there. It's retrievable. It's enjoyable. It's goodly. Better yet, it's godly. If you are without it, look for it. And if you've got it, hold fast to it."

Reading Kevin Leman's new book, *Sheet Music*, you come away with the feeling that sex is God's best work. Because that's what Kevin says. Listen to some comments from his pages.

> *If an atheist ever comes up to you and demands proof*
> *that there is a God, all you have to answer is one word:*
> *"Sex." Give him a day to think about it. If, at the end of*
> *that day, he remains unconvinced, then he has just*
> *revealed far more about his sex life ... or the lack thereof*
> *... than he ever intended.*

> *God created sex. Doesn't that tell you a lot about*
> *who God really is? Among other things, it tells you that*
> *God is truly ingenious.*

Now I have got to tell you, I didn't hear that in church. Oh, I remember them saying that sex was God's good gift. Except that they didn't say it so much as they slid over it on the way to saying other things. And those "other things" drew all kinds of lines around the word "good." And because they talked about the other things so well, they cast all kinds of doubts about the word "good."

I'll never forget the day, along about the seventh grade, when I finally put things together in my head. Prior to that, I knew there was an act identified by a four-letter word written on the walls of the men's room at my school, and described in a very cheap and sleazy novel that Tommy Teeter kept hidden in his bedroom. Yes, I'd heard of that act. But what I didn't know was that there was any connection between that act and how babies got placed in their mommy's tummies. Insofar as I knew, there was this four-letter thing over here, and there was childbirth over there.

And on the day I learned there was a connection, my first thought was not "I can't believe my mother and father did that." Instead, my first thought was: "I can't believe my minister did that." Already, you see, I had gotten the subtle message that while there were many words that could be associated with the word "sex," the word "holy" was not one of them. So how did I get that impression? Either the church taught me that the word "sex" was over here and the word "holy" was over there. Or, if they didn't teach me that in church, it was in the air there. And nobody made any effort to clear the air there.

Well, the Song of Solomon suggests that sex is worthy of God ... worthy of the Bible ... and altogether appropriate for godly, biblical people. And although there are no lines drawn around sex in the Song of Solomon, elsewhere the Bible says: "If you're looking for 'holy,' then marry. Because fun and commitment go hand in hand."

But we've experienced a weird reversal in the culture, to the point that nobody believes what the Bible proclaims ... and what I just said. Today's culture suggests that sex is for everybody but married people. Take television, for example. Do you realize that for the last several years, over 98% of the intimate acts depicted or inferred on television take place between non-married partners? Which demonstrates television's belief that everybody who is not married does it, but that nobody who is married does.

But if that's backward, who says so? Well, married people should say so. And I think many do. But not out loud. For years I have been helping engaged couples come to terms with the marital scripts that have been written for them by their parents. One of those scripts involves marital intimacy. I tell young couples: "Since television will never lead you to believe that married people are intimate, who does tell you, if not your parents?" At which point they look really stupid, as if to say: "Dr. Ritter, that's the dumbest thing anybody has ever said to us." They simply can't picture their parents as being intimate. But believing they know more than they think they know, I quiz them. I don't ask them for answers. But I do force them to face the questions.

1. On a scale of 1 to 10, would you call your parents romantic?

2. On a scale of 1 to 10, would you call your parents sensitive?

3. On a scale of 1 to 10, would you call your parents affectionate?

4. On a scale of 1 to 10, would you call your parents physically demonstrative (in other words, did you grow up in a family of huggers or hand shakers)?

5. When your father buys your mother anniversary gifts, do they always come from Highland Appliance or do they occasionally come from Victoria's Secret?

6. When your mother buys gifts for your father, do they lean in the direction of cashmere sweaters or Sears weed-wackers?

7. What kind of gifts do your parents give each other … personal or practical?

8. What kind of cards do your parents send each other … mushy or funny?

9. What kind of pet names do your parents have for each other…Honey or Bozo?

10. Are your parents "flowers and candy" people, or would buying such things never occur to them?

11. For their 25th, did your parents do Hawaii or Hamtramck?

12. How do your parents function at parties … separated by gender or occasionally together?

13. When your parents walk the beach, do they hold hands or walk 20 feet apart?

14. If nobody else was at home and they were to rent a video from Blockbuster for viewing by firelight, would they be more inclined to rent *Top Gun* or *Sleepless in Seattle*?

15. As concerns the viewing of that same video, would they watch it while sitting on the same piece of furniture or on separate pieces of furniture?

16. Most nights of their married life, do they go to bed at the same time or two hours apart?

17. Do they go to the same room or separate rooms?

18. Do they go to the same bed or separate beds?

19. Can you picture what they wear to bed?

It's fun to watch the lights come on in the brains of 25 year olds when, for the first time, they begin to make sense of the word "intimacy" as connected with 50 year olds.

Clearly, Kevin Leman makes a lucrative living going around the country telling people that sex is godly, sex is goodly, sex is lovely, and that (from personal experience) it is often horribly wasted on the young. I found it interesting that during his visit to Birmingham, he gave four talks, on four subjects, with four titles. But the only title any of you mentioned in conversations with me was his Sunday night title: "Sex Begins in the Kitchen." Sometimes you think I don't listen to you. But I listen better than you think I do.

Which is why I know what you are thinking right now. At least 68.7% of you want me to say: "Yes, but." Then you want me to roll big, long strips of bright yellow "Keep Out" tape (like you see on our construction site) all around everything I've said this morning. Which I have done every other time I have touched on this subject. And which I will do again, relatively soon. In fact, come late spring, you'll absolutely love an entire sermon based on my daughter's answer to a question I posed to her last October when, in response to a discussion that was raging in my Tuesday morning women's group, I said: "Julie, this is what my women want to know. If their unmarried children could banish all concerns about pregnancy and disease, is it possible to have casual, consensual, pleasurable, consequence-free sex?" I'll tease you with her short answer. "No," she said, "but I suppose it depends on how emotionally sterile their children are."

Instead, I leave you with this (which is monumental, given the historic position of much of Christendom ... read that "Roman Catholic Christendom") ... that where intimacy is concerned, the only justification is procreation, never recreation. For pregnancy, always. For pleasure, never.

In response to which Kevin Leman toasted his daughter and son-in-law thusly:

> To my son-in-law, Dennis O'Reilly,
> And his lovely bride, my daughter, Krissy,
> (*wonderful name, by the way*)

Go ahead and create a symphony.

And maybe a few kids, as well.

Kevin, don't you know that half the church thinks you've got that backward?

Fortunately, not my half.

First United Methodist Church
Birmingham, Michigan
February 16, 2003

Notes: In researching this sermon, I turned to multiple commentaries on the Song of Solomon. Therefore, I am quite comfortable in my assertions about what the book is ... and what the book isn't. Surprisingly, the most concise statements came from my beloved Old Testament professor at Yale, B. Davie Napier.

As concerns Kevin Leman, he is an internationally known psychologist, author, and speaker who has written too many books to count. But his most recent effort is marketed under the title Sheet Music: Uncovering the Secrets of Sexual Intimacy in Marriage.

Meanwhile, the book which honored Kris and myself by incorporating our work between its covers, is entitled, "Reflections on Marriage and Spiritual Growth," edited by Andrew Weaver and Carolyn Stapleton.

16

Whose Family Posed for Norman Rockwell?

Scripture: Joshua 24:16-18

This sermon was preached at Northville First UMC during the summer when I was filling the pulpit as an Interim Pastor. It was on this Sunday that I had the privilege of baptizing my first grandchild.

Unless my memory is playing tricks on me ...

1957 was the year

Detroit, the city

Mackenzie, the high school

Eleventh, the grade

American Literature, the subject

Glendora Forshee, the teacher

Poetry, the unit

Robert Frost, Glendoras favorite

(and) memorization, her expectation

Which means that I memorized a lot of Robert Frost in order to pass her class. I may have hated it then. But I am grateful for it now, given that I have immediate recall for lines like:

Home is the place where, when you go there,
they have to take you in.

He is talking about that place, or those people, to whom we turn when it would seem that we have nowhere else to go. When we reach that point where we have no right to go anywhere else or ask anything more, wherever we go next is home. I mean, blood is thicker than water, isn't it? Which suggests that the last door to close in your face will be the door tended by family. When worse comes to worse, we should always be able to go home. At least that is what people say. And that is what many of us do.

Not that homes are always sanctuaries of sweet repose. Truth be told, I suppose every home is dysfunctional (even though I wish we could give that word a rest for the next twenty years of so). Two Sunday mornings ago I slipped into the workroom across from my office for some between service coffee. There were just two mugs available for choosing. Picking up the first, I saw the logo of a local nursing home. Looking in the mirror, I thought, "almost, but not quite." So I put it down and picked up the other. It featured a picture of Bart Simpson saying, "Don't have a cow, man." Whereupon I said, "Not quite, but better." And I poured myself a cup of coffee.

The perfect family is an oxymoron. Maybe the blissfully happy family is too. No family in the Bible fits that description. You can look it up. Although you can also order "The Happy Family Combo" at the New Mandarin Gardens in Farmington Hills. It's a blend of shrimp, scallops, crab, and chicken along with Chinese vegetables served with steamed rice. It's good, but not great. Too much bland. Too little bite.

And speaking of the marriage of happy families and holiday meals, whose family posed for Norman Rockwell anyway? There they are. Heads bowed. Faces scrubbed (all of them bright ... all of them white). Turkey steaming. Grandpa praying. Nobody watching the Dallas Cowboys. Nobody asking, "Why is grandpa taking so long?" Nobody complaining that they don't like turkey, even as somebody else calls, "first dibs on the drumstick." Nobody looking a little red around the eyes because of too many pre-dinner manhattans. Nobody acting up or acting out. Every chair filled. Every head bowed. No empty place where somebody's spouse sat last year but isn't sitting there this year ... because they moved out during the year. And no empty chair that was previously occupied by a teenager who threw a tantrum and refused to come this year (because dinners at grandmas are such a drag). Actually, I do know who posed for that picture. I am talking about the same family that Rockwell painted in a church pew ... all of them holding one hymnal and singing heartily while smiling beatifically.

Well, sometimes it happens just like that. And when it does, it's beautiful. But when it doesn't, it isn't cause to go into mourning. Or hiding. Where we came from is where we came from. And where we are now is where we are now. Airbrushed memories will not help us come to terms with actual realities. Because it is hard to love people when we spend all of our time wishing they were different. Let me say that again. It is hard to love people when we spend all of our time wishing they were different. Especially, when the likelihood of them becoming different is lessened if we do not love them.

Still, if "taking someone in" is the minimum requirement of a home, what might the maximum requirement be? How much dare we hope for from a home? In a world where some would drain the ink cartridge listing many things, while others would simplify matters by boiling it down to one thing, let me suggest three things. In fact, I will make it easier for you by using only words that begin with the letter "M." I am talking about memories, models, and mending.

Let's start with **memories.** At the very minimum, I am talking about the memories we collect. At the maximum, I'm talking about the memories we create. All kinds of people are into collecting memories. Entire industries have grown up around genealogy and scrapbooking. Somebody has got to get it down (the family story I mean). Every family needs its picture takers, journal keepers, tombstone trackers and camcorder operators, along with other family members who can't do any of those things, but who have a way of remembering it all ... including the half you wish they would forget, either because it wasn't true, or because it was all too true.

But creating memories is far more interesting than collecting them, even though it can be tricky. That's because our best intentions can get all messed up. I have a clergy friend who, along with her husband, broke into the piggy bank and took her two daughters (ages eleven and thirteen) to Disney World for the "vacation of a lifetime." Which it was for the eleven-year-old. But it was almost ruined by the thirteen-year-old. The older girl kept reminding everybody "how lame this is" every chance she got. To which anybody can attest who has ever had a kid sit in the car and play video games while overlooking the Grand Canyon.

You can't control that. All you can do is provide experiences and then be open to whatever they yield. Ironically, the experiences that will be best remembered years later will have precious little to do with possessions and purchases. Having mentioned my father in a pair of previous sermons, I can't remember anything specific he ever bought me. But among my most cherished memories are the nights we spent in the rickety bleachers at Butzel Field watching sandlot baseball for the quarter if cost to buy an ice cream bar from the guy in the Good Humor truck.

In fact, I can't think of many possessions (things) that have enriched my life to any significant degree. But I can cite hundreds of experiences that have affected me greatly. Therefore, as I get older, I spend far more dollars on experiences than I do on possessions. I have friends who fail to agree. They say, "Ritter, you blew all that money on a trip, or to pay the ticket scalper three times the face value for some sold-out sporting event. And when it's over, what do you have to show for it?" To which the answer, indeed the only answer, is memories ... especially those I can provide for someone else.

But let me move on to **models**. Preferably, models that work. We are modeling things all the time for our kids. Not all of them are major. I can change a tire because my father once worked in a gas station and I would wander down to the corner to see him in action. What I did not see was him fixing things around the house with tools. So what did my father do around the house? He read books, magazines, newspapers. I never heard him say to me, "Bill, it's far better to read a book than use a tool." But he didn't have to. He modeled it. Not surprisingly, I am inept with tools. Instead, I entered a profession where words become tools. And occasionally, I open my toolbox and use words to fix things.

But there are more important things to model, I suppose. Like marriage and faith. I once said in a sermon that the most important thing a father could teach his son is how to love a woman, with a similar admonition to mothers about how to love a man. And while that may have a bit of a "dated" ring to it, I am willing to stand by it.

Somebody has to teach us about life's most intimate relationships, and one of the best ways to do it is by example.

Which also includes a relationship with God. Over and over again, I've preached a funeral for an aged parent, of whom the adult children have said, "Mom wasn't what you would call religious, but she was truly a good woman." Or, "Dad wasn't what you would call the church-going type, but we never heard him say a bad word about anybody."

Which is not to be sneezed at. We need good women. Just as we need men who hold their tongues. But one wonders if dad ever said a good word about anybody … or to anybody. Did dad ever stand up to anybody, or for anything? And as for mom (the "good woman"), how many extra miles did she go? How much forgiving did she do? And to what degree was wound-binding, burden-baring, and peace-making part of her nature? And if reconciliation is the heart of the Gospel … "God was in Christ reconciling the world unto himself and entrusting unto us this ministry of reconciliation" … how many bridges did mom or dad ever build over the troubled waters of fractured relationships? After all, the Christian faith is more than keeping your lawn mowed and your nose out of other peoples' business. And if those same kids could also tell me a few of mom's favorite Bible verses or dad's favorite hymns, it would tell me more about that family than newspapers would ever include in any obituary. What did we read just minutes ago? "As for me and my house, we will serve the Lord." So said Joshua. Or maybe it was Mrs. Joshua.

Having talked about memories and models, let's turn to **mending**. That's right, mending. I am not talking about the kind you do with needle and thread. Fewer and fewer of us do that kind of mending anymore. Talking with a retired home economics teacher recently, I learned that schools haven't taught sewing in years. Who knew? But, then, I doubt there are five people in this congregation who ever darn socks anymore.

You have probably realized I am not talking about the mending that takes place when clothing gets ripped. I am talking about the mending that needs to take place when people get ripped. Given that not every place will take us in a ripped condition. Some places, even some churches, are glad to have us, only when we have it all together. But don't all of us long for places to go when we are in pieces? Listen to this:

> *When I was in the sixth grade, there was an election for captain of the safety patrol. I loved the idea of wearing the uniform and was determined to be captain. But when the vote came in, I'd lost to another kid by a margin of 22-20. I was bitterly disappointed. The following day, while watching Tom Mix movies at the Saturday matinee, I sat behind the biggest kid in our class. He turned around, saw me and said, "You dumb Wop. You lost the election." "I know," I said, "but why call me dummy?" "Because," he said, "There are only 38 kids in our class, and 42 voted. Can't you Dagos even count?" I went to the*

*teacher and told her that some kids had voted twice. All she said was, "That's a shame, but since it's over and done with, let's leave well enough alone."*5

So who was that "Dago"? Lee Iacocca, that's who. And where did he go when his innocence got shattered, and his trusting view of the world fell apart in the sixth grade? He went home to have his heart sewed up. "Mending," was what his mama called it.

•••••••

Memories, models, and mending. That's enough for you to digest this morning. So how about if I close with a word just for my grandson.

Jacob, ten years prior to the day of your birth … although I had no way of knowing that that date would become your actual birthday … your grandmother and I left for Israel with 48 of our nearest and dearest. And after baptizing some of those folk in the River Jordan (where Jesus was baptized), I filled a small plastic bottle with river water just for you. I figured I would have a grandchild someday … somewhere … somehow. Actually, that's not quite true. I knew the "somehow" part. But I also knew that life comes with no guarantees. Which is why, ten years later, your birth (in a blizzard) was incredibly special. Now, following three days of labor and twenty-three weeks of life, you are here … in church … in a Christening gown my father wore in 1909, I wore in 1940, and your mother wore in 1975. But, as ancestry goes, you've got relatives, on your father's side, who came to America on the Mayflower. Indeed, the very first child born on that ship was Oceanus Hopkins. But water from the Jordan trumps both

Baptism of Jacob Ritter Hopkins

your gown and your Pilgrim heritage because it links you to Jesus ... and His baptism ... and His love for little children ... and His love for you.

I think it was Margaret Mead who first said, "It takes a village to raise a child." But there are some of us who think those odds increase if that village has a church in it.

Sad to say, I know people who made it to the front of the church only twice in their lives. And they were carried in both times. Last Sunday, your grandmother carried you down front as she took Communion. Unfortunately, for you, we weren't serving rice cereal. But I pray there will come a day when you walk to the front of the church to sing a song, get a Bible, confirm your faith, or become recognized as a graduate. And maybe, if your grandmother and I eat enough oat bran, we might even live long enough to see you commit your life to another (I am talking about "better-worse, richer-poor, to love and to cherish"). And if, after your quarterbacking days are over, God were to mug you or nudge you in the direction of some church's pulpit, I'll save my old sermons.

But this morning, it's not about who you will become. This morning is about who you are right now.

A child of God

A sign of hope

An answer to prayer

A sweet and utterly charming little boy

And a source of great joy to a family that loves you very much

First United Methodist Church
Northville, Michigan
August 12, 2007

17

From the Jordan to Georgia

This meditation was shared in a lovely chapel located in a historic setting in the town where we now live and worship. Our extended family had come together for the baptism of our granddaughter.

My Lord, what a morning. Bright, clear, and filled with promise. Georgia Grace Hopkins being the reason we are here. It is the morning of her baptism in this historic chapel. Parents and grandparents are here. Aunts and uncles are here. Cousins, too. Why not ... of course they're here. Georgia's older brother, Jacob ... he's here as well. Along with a few dear friends to flesh out the congregation. And with a veritable "cloud of witnesses," especially if you include those who have gone before us, but who (in ways that exceed our human understanding) may be looking down on us, so as to be numbered among us.

Grandpa Joe's job this morning has been to give us music. Which he has done beautifully. While my job, or I'd rather call it my high honor, is to celebrate the sacrament. But on the way to the font, I am heeding Julie and Jared's expectation when they said, "Of course you'll say a few words." Which I have come prepared to do, grouping those words under a trio of headings.

Names.

Among my post-retirement jobs is one as a ghostwriter for a bank president. And among my regular assignments are articles that I write (over his name) for his corporate newsletter. Just last week I wrote about a change in the bank's corporate name, following a merger by acquisition of Citizen's First Bank of Port Huron. Struggling to embrace their new corporate identity, many of his Port Huron employees weren't using the bank's new name. Said my friend, "I recognize their reluctance. Change is hard. I know that. But our name is important to us, and we need our new employees to embrace it. After all, it's our brand." Tongue in cheek, I suggested a bank baptism in the St. Clair River under the Blue Water Bridge. I pictured myself asking the board of directors: "By what name shall we call this bank?" I even suggested that we might immerse several of the bank's managers. But when my friend failed to see the humor in my suggestion, I quickly dismissed it.

Names are important. Speaking personally, I like my newest one. In this family, I am now known as "Boppa," married to "Neena." Who decided that it should be so? Jacob decided that it should be so. And Jacob is Georgia's old brother by two and a half years. I know he likes his name. Ask him and he will not only speak it but spell it. "My name is J A C O B … I'm Jacob."

But not everyone feels similarly. Years ago I laid my hand on a kid's head and confirmed him. His first name was Brian. His last name was Horr. Last week I officiated at his wedding. When I met the couple for counseling, he said, "I've changed my name." "You mean I should no longer call you Brian?" I asked. "No, it's not my first name I changed. It's my last name. It's no longer 'Horr.' It's 'Harr.'" "What's up with that?" I wondered. "Well," he said, "since you last saw me I have graduated from med school and am now making rounds in hospitals. And I hate hearing the loudspeakers in the hallways saying, "Paging Dr. Horr, paging Dr. Horr.'"

In baptism, we ask: "By what name shall we call this child?" My maternal grandmother was born in Yugoslavia. Of six children born to her parents, she was the only girl. She was given the name "Agnes." Her family name was "Potokor." She claimed she had no middle name. But all of her life in this country she celebrated two special days. The first, January 20, was her birthday. The other day she called her Name Day. I have long since forgotten the actual date. But her name day was the day of her baptism. Because, as she claimed, a child's name was given (I mean, literally given) at baptism. Before your name day, you were simply known as "baby."

Georgia Grace is this child's name. She is named after her late great-grandmother. Georgia Haerr Larson. I am talking about Kris' mother and my mother-in-law. Just the other day I saw Georgia Grace playing in the dirt. In her mind, she was planting. Kris' mother was also at home in the dirt. Coming from farm roots in Ohio, she earned a horticulture degree at MSU and later ran a nursery. She knew each of her roses by two names, Latin and English. And more than once I heard her walk through a garden and say, "And how's Mr. Lincoln doing this morning?"

Kris' mother was a groundbreaker in a lot of ways. She left the farm, got her degree, heading first to Temple University in Philadelphia before transferring to Michigan State. She loved to regale us with details of animal dissection in the laboratory, never failing to point out the number of male students who were unwilling to participate. The route she took to her degree was only minimally understood by her family. And years later, when she was pursuing a master's degree in education, she actually left home and husband for an entire summer and took up residence in a college dormitory at Eastern Michigan University. And when I came along at age 23 to court her then-17-year-old daughter, she didn't throw me off the porch. I think she secretly wanted Kristine to marry a minister. And as clergy were concerned, she eventually said (following the death of her husband), "I think I'll marry one too." And at age 70, she did.

In addition to dirt loving and groundbreaking, she was also a reader, a traveler, a church goer, a school board member and, at every level imaginable, a teacher. So if Georgia Grace turns out to be anything like her, I expect we will soon see her playing Uno, planting roses, and plowing through books like *Stalking the Wild Asparagus.*

So knowing where the name "Georgia" comes from, you might be wondering about "Grace." When I asked Kris, she said, "Darned if I know. I don't remember any 'Grace' in our family." But from time to time there was. And it was truly amazing.

Scripture tells us that God knows our name. Which is an incredible claim when you think about it. One of my favorite spirituals begins: "Hush, hush, somebody's calling my name." And my friend Barry Johnson, an incredibly gifted preacher, is fond of saying:

Georgia Grace Hopkins

"Each of us is a unique, unrepeatable miracle of creation." Which seems to be a good thing to remember about all of us in this room, not the least of which is Georgia Grace.

Names. **Promises.**

In short order, Jared and Julie will make some promises as parents. And we will make another promise as a congregation. But God makes one, too. And God's promise is, "I will love what I have made." But to be truthful, it should be restated to say, "I do love what I have made." God's love is not launched by this service. It does not begin when this water is applied by this preacher. God's promise has been active from the very beginning ... from Georgia's very beginning. I can't tell you how many young parents have been pressured (usually by grandparents) to "get this child done." Followed by "get her done quickly." They are talking about baptism. But behind the pressure to "get it done soon" is an unspoken fear. When pressed as to their feeling of urgency, they respond, "What if something happens?" What they are really saying is, "What if this dear child were to die in an unbaptized state?" Will he or she then fall outside the grace of God? But the thing they really worry about but never say out loud, is, "Will this unbaptized child go to hell?" So I seek to reassure them by saying, "Baptism does not launch God's love. Baptism points to God's love. Because God's love has been there from the very beginning. Better yet, it has been there from Georgia Grace's very beginning.

Names. Promises. **Water.**

I will baptize Georgia Grace with water. I will use only a small amount. I have hand-carried this water all the way from the Jordan River. Yes, you really can get Jordan River water through customs. Actually, I have entered the Jordan and baptized several adults by immersion. But the amount of water does not alter the sacrament. Neither does the source of the water. "Holy water" is neither a matter of volume, nor origin. And it certainly is not a matter of chemistry. The specialness of Jordan River water has less to do with where I got it than with the fact that I brought it (along with the story that goes with it).

Georgia Grace loves her bath. Water makes her happy. Water also makes her clean.

From dirt.

From spit-up.

From other bodily secretions.

And also from sin.

But most of us have a hard time associating the word "sin" with the word "baby." There was once a grandmother who said to me on a baptism Sunday, "You can't tell me that a sweet, adorable child like this has ever done anything bad in her whole life." To which I responded, "Maybe so, grandma. But give her time."

I should have added that baptismal water cleanses, renews and washes things away. Like sin. Some of us remember the phrase, "That's water over the dam." Which means that we are not going to remain locked in the past, or in the sins of the past. Rather, we will be jumpstarted toward the future. The waters of baptism carry sins over the dam. Not that we need to rush down to the church ... or to the river ... every time we sin. No, doing it once carries the suggestion that the merciful flow goes on.

That is unless we humans fortify the dam so that no cleansing water can flow over it. I have no doubt that my mother loved me. Nor do I have any doubt that she was proud of me. But the only two stories I ever remember her telling about my birth and early childhood might have given me reason to wonder. Her only birth story involved how long my birth took, how hard it was, and how much pain I caused her. Every time she told it (usually in the company of others), I felt like I should apologize. Her other story concerned the night she was all dressed up to go somewhere, and I spit up all over her dress. People would laugh, and I would cringe, until one day in my mid-thirties I said, "But I promise never to do it again."

A lot of people are burdened by others who seem to remember all of their sins, their faults, their failings, and their shortcomings. These people can both recall and recite everything they ever did wrong, when they did it, how many times they did it, and how much trouble it caused when they did it. If you have some of those people in your life, you find yourself wishing they would develop amnesia … maybe even a mild case of Alzheimer's. To such people, we cry, "Can't you let it go?" Well, God can let it go. The gospel proclaims it. Water symbolizes it. And the best news is that while God can let **it** go, God cannot let **us** go.

> *Georgia Grace,*
> *This may be the last time I ever lay my hands on*
> *you liturgically.*
> *I may not live long enough to*
> > *confirm you,*
> > *to marry you,*
> > *or to ordain you.*
> *But I will continue to speak a good word to you and for*
> *you.*
> *And I will always …*
> > *Hold you close.*
> > *Cheer you on.*
> > *Pray you up.*
>
> *And love you from the bottom of my heart.*
>
> *E -I -E -I -O*

Northville Mill Race Chapel
Northville, Michigan
2010

18

What to Do With Your Brown Bag

Scripture: Matthew 11:25-30

This is the only sermon in this collection where I am not identifiable by name. But don't be fooled. I am in there somewhere. As are most of you.

Let's begin with Zan Holmes ... down Texas way ... who recalls an incident from his younger days in an earlier church.

> We had a little dog in those years, a rather undisciplined terrier who answered to the name of "Brownie." And since our parsonage was in a rather heavily trafficked part of town, we didn't figure it was safe to let Brownie run free in the yard. So we attached his collar to a length of chain ... and attached the chain to a pole in the center of the yard. That way, if Brownie wanted to run (which was every time a human being

was sniffed or sighted), he would race round and round the pole, with the length of his chain defining the outer limits of his mobility. In fact, the circle in which he traveled became so familiar that no grass would grow where Brownie ran.

Then one day I looked out the window and discovered that, as most chains eventually do, this chain had snapped. There was Brownie ... free at last ... running for everything he was worth ... in the same old familiar circles. He was free and didn't know it. Why? Because he was still hung up on his past hang-ups.

As are a lot of us. Many of us have come this morning, still tethered to pieces of our past ... to the degree that free and unhindered motion remains a virtual impossibility.

Some of us are tethered to scars from the past that will not heal. Life has wounded us. Love has wounded us. Enemies have hurt us plenty. Friends (and sometimes family) have hurt us more. That thick skin we show the world ... it's scar tissue. Behind it can be found a litany of betrayals. People who said one thing and did another. People who said good things but did worse things. People who went back on their word. People who weren't as good as their word. People who came upon us in moments of desperate need, and spoke not a word. And people who lied.

Much of which was awful when it happened. And some of which became more awful with each passing year. That's because some of us have nursed our wounds ... never quite letting them scab over ... but occasionally picking away at them, the better to watch them bleed. To be sure, wounds cannot heal until they bleed. But I've never heard anyone make a case suggesting that healing accelerates with multiple re-bleedings.

Some people rehearse the same crimes and misdemeanors over and over, telling them to anyone who will listen. It becomes part of their story ... their explanation ... their excuse ... for not having gotten on with it (whatever "it" was that needed getting on with ... job ... friendship ... marriage ... life). "Why haven't I seen you suited up and out on life's playing field?" I ask. To which you answer: "I've been hurt, you know. You don't expect me to play hurt, do you?"

Meanwhile, others of us are tethered by sins from the past that will not fade. Once upon a time, we did something. Which made us feel bad. Or we kept on doing the same thing. Which made us feel worse. I've heard a lot of sophisticated definitions of sin in my time, including some I have written myself. But I can never quite dismiss the kid in my first youth group who threw his two cents into the theological hopper when he said: "Sin? I guess sin is what I feel bad after."

Sometimes our sins are discovered. Sometimes not. Which may be worse. Because sin that is kept hidden from public sight often moves to the forefront of private mind ... where it becomes the stuff of secret shame, crippling guilt or a self-image that is pitted by spiritual acne.

"I'm not as good as you think I am, Reverend."

"If you really knew me, you wouldn't want me in your church."

People really say such things. Some in jest. But many in earnest. Among my most difficult conversations are those that begin with someone saying: "For as long as you've known me, Bill, there are things you don't know about me."

Old scars! Old sins! Sometimes, time tricks us so that we're not even sure where we got them ... or how long we've had them. Some of us even think we hide them pretty well. But they slip out. Among the Christmas letters we got one year was one from an old friend, now largely distanced from our lives. She is divorced. Kids are grown. Grandchildren are coming. She has travels to take and tales to tell. All of which she told ... that Christmas ... in her letter. But the letter went on longer than most do. And the words became more bitter than most are. For what was being rehearsed (paragraph upon painful paragraph) was the divorce. What caused it. Who caused it. Who did what. Who said what. Who made off with what. Who was (or was not) left with what ... when the ink was dry on the settlement. And it's been quite a while since the ink was dry. The divorce is relatively old news.

As to whether her letter was all scars ... or whether there were some sins in there, too ... I do not know. All I know is that she didn't sit down to write that letter ... didn't think she'd sent that letter ... and would be surprised if she knew how the rest of us read that letter. That's because, all things considered, she thinks she's doing well. Which she is. And yet ...

••••••••

You've noticed, of course, that when people come to the start of the new year ... a new job ... a new semester ... or a new phase in their life ... their talk turns to the making of resolutions. Clean page time. Fresh start time. Each January 2, there are more people in the locker room of my athletic club than any other week. It's that way every January. All's well that starts well. Yet when you read the cartoons and comic strips shortly after New Year's, you'll be amazed to discover how many story lines focus on the utter futility of bothering to resolve anything. It is as if they are saying: "What's the use? After all, we are who we are. We do what we do. We bring what we bring. What you see is what you get."

Well, I suppose there's something to be said for realism. But before you accommodate yourselves to the future by settling too quickly for too little, let me tell you a story.

Once upon a time, there was a man who carried a brown bag virtually everywhere he went. No one knew where the bag came from. But there were some who said that his carrying of it went back a long way, maybe even to his cradle. When he was a child, he hung onto the brown bag wherever he went. Kids at school would tease him about it. And more than one teacher suggested that he leave it in his locker. But he steadfastly hung onto it, as if it were an indispensable part of his existence.

When he was in high school, he went out for football ... and was actually known to have carried his brown bag into the huddle. The coach said: "Do that one more time, and you'll never play for me again." So he forced himself to leave it on the bench. But not without warning everybody against touching it, and placing it in a visible spot in order to make certain no one did. No one knew what was in the brown bag. But neither had anyone seen him without it. He took it with him everywhere, even on dates. As close as any girl ever got to him on the front seat of the car, the brown bag was closer.

As he became an adult, there was less talk about his bag. He still carried it. People could still see it. But politeness led almost everyone to ignore it. And he became a bit more sophisticated about it, to the point of occasionally slipping it into his briefcase or tucking it under his coat. Still, on his wedding day, he carried it down the aisle with him. Black tux. Black tie. Black shoes. Brown bag. But who would have expected otherwise? After all, he took his bag everywhere. Off to work. Out to play. Down to the basement. Up to bed. It was the one thing he never checked when he went to the airport. And it was the only thing he never forgot when leaving the house. One night, after a couple too many pina coladas, his wife said: "You're going to carry that brown bag to your grave." But what she was actually wondering was whether he would look unnatural if she laid him out without it in his casket.

One day, in his late forties, he left his office at lunchtime, feeling the need to go for a walk. Which was how he came to pass the church that was offering a mid-day service for time-crunched office workers. Not quite knowing why, he found himself walking in. And not quite knowing what to do, he found himself sitting down. The fact that the minister was getting up to preach made him moderately grateful that he wouldn't have to stay a long time, and extremely grateful that he wouldn't have to sing. But when the minister opened the Bible and read, "Come unto me, all ye that labor and are heavy laden, and who carry a brown bag," he inched forward to hear whatever might be coming next, even as he began to fidget (unconsciously, and more than a little nervously) with his own brown bag.

The minister talked, both warmly and wisely, about the burdens most of us carry through life. Then he said: "Any of you who labor and are heavy laden, and who carry a brown bag, are welcome to leave your burdens (and your bag) on the altar." Which, surprisingly, several people did. And for the very first time in his life, the man noticed that a lot of other people were carrying brown bags, too.

So timidly at first (and then hurriedly ... as if to get it over with before he chickened out), he headed for the altar. Which, by now, was piled high with bags. When he got there, he stood for a long time ... bag in hand ... not quite certain what he wanted (or was ready) to do. Finally, he let it go ... left it behind ... and went.

Walking back down the aisle, he was surprised by how good he felt. And walking out of the church, he was amazed at feeling better still. He felt so good that he wanted to shout. But shouting was not his style. So he settled for clapping his hands together. And he couldn't believe how easily he could clap, once he no longer had to lay his brown bag aside in order to be able to do so. Later on, he found the same to be true for a lot of things ... like working ... waving ... hugging ... and praying.

••••••••

"Come unto me, all ye who labor and are heavy laden ... and who carry a brown bag. And I will give you rest."

Brown bags represent a lot of things in our culture. Children use them to carry sandwiches to school. Winos use them to carry bottles of cheap muscatel from curb to curb. Homeless ladies use them to carry their worldly goods from shelter to shelter. And recently, in beautiful downtown Clawson, I saw a lingerie store named "Brown Bag It," and found myself wondering what kind of lingerie one might buy ... and for whom ... that would best be carried from the premises in a brown bag.

But you know that's not the brown bag I'm talking about. And you've also figured out why there's a brown bag inserted in your worship bulletin this morning. It's there to remind us that we all carry one … and that most of us are looking for somewhere to leave it. We've tried ignoring it. We've tried hiding it. Some of us have tried showing the contents of our bag to other members of our family … in hopes that they might take out of the bag some of the stuff we figure they put into it in the first place. But not only wouldn't they take anything out, they wouldn't let us get out the door until they'd put more stuff in. And some of us have even tried dropping our bags and running, only to have the finders come running after us, thinking we would reward them for their diligence.

But it doesn't have to be that way. It really doesn't. There is some place you can leave it, knowing that it will be carried for you. I don't know what you may be carrying into this church today. I don't know all of your scars and sins. Neither do I know all of the ways in which you have been wounded, bruised or short-changed by life. All I can offer is a gospel that says you don't have to carry what you can't carry. So if you want to use the bag in your bulletin as a means of responding to what the gospel offers, it's all right with me.

So why not take that bag and put some of your burdens inside it, this very morning. Sins. Wounds. Painful memories. Unresolved conflicts. Whatever. Stuff 'em in there. Maybe you'll want to take out a pen or a pencil and write your burden on the bag itself. Then fold it. No one will read it. Ever. I promise.

In a moment, Jan Albright is going to sing the gospel's promise. Then we're going to sing a hymn. And if (during the solo or the hymn) you want to bring your bag forward and put it in one of these big bags in the front of the chancel, feel free to do so. Jan won't mind. Neither will anybody else. Or if you can't bring yourself to do that … yet still have a bag you want to leave at the church … come up after the service when no one is looking. And if the whole idea seems hokey, ask yourself: "Is it the mechanics of leaving my bag which make me uncomfortable, or is it the idea of letting it go?"

Later, I am going to collect the big bag. I am going to bring it to the altar. I am going to pray over it. Then I am going to burn it. On Ash Wednesday, when we have our fourteen-hour, come-and-go Communion Services, some of those ashes will be available, should anyone want to use them. That way, they will become a sign (however briefly) of the burdens that we are supposed to carry for each other.

"Come unto me, all ye who labor and are heavy laden … and who carry a brown bag. For you will find rest unto your souls."

Note: The "Brown Bag" story is obviously apocryphal. I don't have the faintest idea where it originated. I first happened upon it, courtesy of a tip provided by Carl Price. My primary source is Thomas Lane Butts, a gifted colleague and friend who preaches in Alabama. But Tom admits that the story didn't originate with him, either. Who knows where it originated? It circulates because it is good. And because it is true. Which is why I stole it. In point of fact, most preachers are thieves. The secret lies in learning to steal "good stuff."

First United Methodist Church
Birmingham, Michigan
June 12, 2005

19

Our Place

Scripture: Genesis 28:10 17

In retirement, I have preached this sermon more than once. But never was I touched more personally than doing it at Nardin Park for their 50th in the present sanctuary.

This is a week of grand occasions. A golden sanctuary anniversary today. President's Day tomorrow. Valentine's Day yesterday. And Scout Sunday, last Sunday. As concerns Scout Sunday, I doubt you celebrated it. It's not the big thing it used to be. But I can still remember the late George Thomas insisting that we not only needed to do it, but that we were going to do it. And I agreed, given that I had once walked the scouting trail all the way from Cubs to Explorers. And I suspect I had plenty of company, including many of you.

So okay! Everybody ready! Those of you who know the Scout Law, say it with me: "A Scout is trustworthy … loyal … helpful … friendly … courteous … kind … obedient … cheerful … thrifty … brave … clean … reverent." Like riding a bicycle, once you learn it, you never forget it.

Unfortunately, we used to race through it as kids, seeing how fast we could say it. We said the Scout Law like the Catholic kids in our neighborhood used to say their "Hail Mary's." They figured if the priest required them to say seven, they wanted to spit them out as quickly as possible.

How did I learn that? I learned that from the Burghardt brothers (who were the only Catholic boys in our Methodist Scout Troop). They were the ones who taught me about rapid-fire Hail Mary's. Which may explain why we countered with rapid-fire recitals of the Scout Law. But no matter how rapidly we said it, we always landed hard on the word "reverent." If we could make it to "reverent," the race was finished. Once we'd said it, who cared whether we could explain it? Although, even at that young age, I was thinking about becoming a "Reverend."

Which is a weird title, don't you know. The word "reverent" is an adjective, not a noun. And it certainly isn't a title. But people think I need a title. They get all hung up over what to call me. I tell them to go with "Bill." But, for a lot of them, that's not holy enough. And "Father" doesn't work, except from my daughter, Julie. In the South, I'd be

"Preacher," as in "Preacher Bill," or "Brother Billy." If I were Lutheran, I'd be "Pastor Bill." If I were an Episcopalian, I could have my pick of titles. I could be "Curate," "Vicar," "Rector," or even "Coadjutor" or "Suffragan." The word "Doctor" strokes my ego, even though it's mostly honorary. But "Reverend" is where most people settle, so I'll own it ... wear it ... do what I can to live up to it ... even in a world that has trouble explaining it.

So I am a "Reverend," who may or may not be "reverent." But what does that mean? I could answer by reading from the dictionary. Or I could tell you a couple of stories. For better or worse, I have chosen to go with the stories. The first of which is generically true ... meaning that it could have happened to any one of you. And maybe it did.

You are about 12 or 13 ... old enough to wander without somebody wondering where you have wandered off to. Sometimes, you wandered with friends. But sometimes, you wandered alone. And once, while wandering alone, you got a little bit off the beaten path. And then you got a whole lot off the beaten path. But you weren't lost ... either because you were too preoccupied to be lost ... too confident in your abilities to be lost ... or because it was too early in the day to be lost. Very few people get lost at 11:00 in the morning. Most people realize they are lost about supper time (or when the sun goes down).

Which is how it came to pass that you stumbled upon a place you had never been before. Indeed, it seemed as if nobody had ever been there before. It was secluded without being scary … quiet without being eerie. "Still," was what it was. "Calm," too. "Peaceful" … definitely peaceful. And maybe even "lovely" … although never in your life had you said the word "lovely" before … and wouldn't (for the life of you) want anyone to hear you saying it now.

And maybe the reason it was so … whatever it was … was the view. Maybe you looked out from a clearing … or over a ledge … and it seemed as if the whole world was opening up to you. Or maybe you couldn't see anything much at all, given that you were surrounded by trees. Except that here and there, there were cracks in the foliage, so that little slices of sunlight knifed through and made this incredible pattern where they crossed. Then you could sit in the middle of that pattern (literally feeling the sun's warmth on your skin). Or you could sit just off to the side, watching the pattern change (minute by minute) as the sun moved this way or that.

Finally, after staying far longer than you intended, you left. But before leaving, you covered every trace of your having been there. On the way home, you took special pains to remember how to get back. And you went back … a surprising number of times. Not really to do anything there. But because you liked how it felt there. And you liked how you felt there. You always went by yourself. Though every now and again, you had this crazy idea … it was crazy, wasn't it? … that you weren't actually alone there.

One day, you told your best friend about the place, swearing him to secrecy. But your friend told somebody else and, pretty soon, there were four of your friends demanding that you take them to your special place. And without quite knowing why, you almost led them astray, pretending that you no longer remembered the way.

But you got there. And you got them there. Whereupon, one looked around and said" "So ...?" And another said: "What's the big deal?" Even as a third said: "You dragged us all the way out here for this?" While the fourth, who said nothing, walked over to the place you usually sat and began relieving himself against a tree. After that, you never went back to that place again. Because it wasn't the same anymore.

Which brings me to my second story ... one that is not so much generically true, as personally true. Meaning that it happened to me. Not so very long ago, Kris and I went to a wedding. Which is to say we attended a wedding. I did not perform the wedding. Meaning that I did not stand up here (in a robe) looking like me, but sat down there (in a suit) looking like you. Like in a pew. Where I do not hang out very often. Meaning that I do not know what it is like ... out there ... where you are.

The wedding was for a friend. It was not for my friend's kid. It was for my friend. Who is my age. Meaning that it was important to me. Because my friend is important to me. His first wife - who was also my friend – had died of cancer. I buried her. Now he had found another, or another had found him. I was happy for them both.

Anyway, Kris and I took our places in the pew ... right down there ... in this very church ... a most beautiful church ... with a beautiful organ ... playing beautiful music ... for a crowd of beautiful people ... who were behaving (for the most part) beautifully. Yes, beautifully. Except for the people immediately behind me. They were listening to nothing and talking about everything ... including a lot of talking about hunting. And as the wedding got closer and closer their talk got louder and louder. Whereupon I leaned over to Kris and whispered (very quietly), "is it always like this out here?" To which she whispered back (even more quietly), "More than you know."

I found myself wanting to turn and glare, ever so briefly, at the people behind me. And up until a few years ago, I would have. Because, until a few years ago, I was in that period in my life when I would occasionally count items in the grocery carts of people in the "express checkout lines" and kindly point out to them that this was a "12 items or less" line, and they had 27 items in their cart (33, when I counted the cans in the six-pack separately). But I didn't turn and glare because, now that I am older and wiser, I realize that no one died and appointed me "Lord of the Universe." So I sat facing forward, grinding my teeth in silence.

My friend's adult children began processing. Whereupon my tears began rolling. And the organ began swelling. Which was when it happened.

But before I tell you what happened, I need to remind you that this church ... is dominated (architecturally) by the floor-to-ceiling window of stained glass. I mean the whole front of the church is a window. It's not a window in the wall. The window is the wall. And it's mostly of Jesus (although the disciples are in it, too).

So there I was ... forward facing ... tears welling ... family coming ... organ swelling ... when the man behind me talking (subject, hunting) noticed the window for the very first time. I mean, we'd been sitting there for 15 minutes. How could he have missed it before this? But, seeing it now, he pointed it out to his significant (female) other. Then, in a stage whisper, he said: "Wow. I wonder what a .357 Magnum would do to that?" To which she said, "It would send you straight to hell."

Now I know the guy was just being funny. I don't think he was planning on blowing out the window. And I don't think he was planning on blowing out Jesus. I mean, Jesus has been killed before. And I'm not sure anybody went "straight to hell" for that, either ... given that it is in God's nature to be far more merciful than I would ever think of being.

No, the guy behind me wasn't so much sinful as stupid. Or

Nardin Park United Methodist Church sanctuary

insensitive. Or inappropriate. He just said the first thing that came into his head. And it's a free country. You can pretty much say anything to anyone, at any time, in any place ... except "fire" in a crowded theater. But I wanted to turn around, shake his lapels, and say to him: "Look, buddy, if this place ... if this window ... if this figure ... if this moment ... if these lovers ... if none of this means anything to you ... can you tell me what, if anything, does?"

I mean, at some point in your life, you are going to have an experience for which no other word will suffice except the word "sacred." And it's going to touch you ... move you ... humble you. Moreover, it's going to shut your ever-loving mouth ... bring a tear to your eye ... form a lump in your throat ...drag a long, slow sigh from your lungs ... and maybe even drop you to your knees. Whereupon, you may attempt to explain what has happened with traditional words like "God" or "Jesus" or "church" or "sanctuary." But, more likely, you will not know what words to use, although later you may say with Jacob: "Surely the Lord was in this place and I didn't even know it."

What it means to be "reverent" is to look for those moments ... to be open to them when they come ... to give space to others to experience them wherever they find them. And, then, when they happen to you, it is to say: "This is as good as it gets ... as true as it gets ... as close to the heart of things as it gets ... and maybe even as holy as it gets" (even though "holy" is another of those words like "lovely," and this is the first time you ever found yourself daring to speak it with your lips).

Ok, it's time to make this timely. You know why I am here? I am here because this place is both lovely and holy ... and, over 50 years you have sacrificed to make it so, historically and financially.

Fifty years is a long time. Yes, there was another Nardin Park before this one. It was located at 5151 West Chicago, just a few miles from where I grew up. I worshiped there once or twice. I played basketball there … went to District youth activities there … and, in the 13 years I was here, actually went back and preached in the pulpit on West Chicago.

I go back a lot further with Nardin Park than most of you know. Go out in the hallway leading to the Memorial Garden and look at the pastors whose pictures are hanging there. I have known all of them but two. One of them, Marshall Reed, left Nardin Park, became a bishop, and (in 1963) ordained me as a Deacon. Several years later, I buried his widow. Verner Mumbulo and I co-officiated his granddaughter, Karen Hildebrand's wedding here. Verner and I also ate English muffins and studied the Bible together every Saturday morning here. I buried him, too. And years later, Maud, his wife. And I will never forget my friend, Bill Mercer, who I followed here. I buried him, too.

For thirteen years (1980-1993) Kris and I lived here, served here, raised Bill and Julie here, and made tons of friends here. I preached somewhere in the vicinity of 575 sermons here, coupled with approximately 1,200 weddings, funerals, and baptisms here. I also did a bit of building and remodeling here; survived an embezzlement here, raised no small amount of money here, and felt Jesus become close and personal here.

Amazing things have happened in sanctuaries like this one. Several years ago, I was watching Wolf Blitzer (that's what I need, a name like

"Wolf Blitzer"). He was covering the West Virginia mine disaster. Let me set the scene. Blitzer was in a CNN newsroom. But there was a live reporter on the scene standing, microphone in hand, in front of the Sago Baptist Church. A white church. A frame church. You've seen one, you've seen a lot of them. No big deal from the outside. But suddenly, a very big deal on the inside. Because that's where the families of the trapped miners were, and where the cameras weren't ... because the cameras weren't allowed. Suddenly, Blitzer said to the reporter, "So, Brittany (or Kimberly, or Katie, whomever), do you know what goes on in there? I mean, are they praying, singing, holding hands?" Well, I suppose a lot of people wonder what goes on in places like this. So let me ask you. Aren't you glad to be numbered among the portion of the population that knows the answer to Wolf Blitzer's question (about what goes on in places like this, I mean)?

There's something about a place like this that not only tells us what to do, but also tells us who we are. Something that defines us, so that we can never fall victim to identity theft.

Allow me to take you, as I close, to a scene from what Terry Lawson called "An absolutely wonderful movie that hardly anybody saw." Called *Junebug*, it tells the story of a young man from rural North Carolina who moves to a big city (Chicago), where he reinvents himself, conveniently forgetting the family which birthed him, raised him, but now mostly embarrasses him. Attending an art auction in the Windy City, he beds, then weds, an utterly charming and sophisticated art dealer with origins in Great Britain. Three months later, he accompanies his new wife on a buying trip to North Carolina, where he reluctantly agrees to her request that "while we're here, we should go meet your family."

He hasn't been home in three years. And upon arriving, it is apparent that the discrepancies of class and style are enormous. But his bride deals with them better than he does. And then one night they accompany his family to a covered-dish supper at the local church. Now I've got to tell you that after fifty years of church potlucks, the filmmaker caught this one perfectly. Even though I hadn't brought a dish, I was all set to take my plate, grab Kris and get in line. Heck, I'd have given the invocation in exchange for a chance to go first.

After supper, there's a bit of fellowship time. During which the preacher says: "Folks, we sure are excited to see George (along with his new wife) back among us after such a long time in that big city up North. Why I'll bet we can even coax him up here to sing for us, like we remember him doing so many times before he left."

Which embarrasses him. But what can he do? So he comes up front. Another guy in overalls comes up to sing bass. A teenager (the son of the bass) slides in to sing tenor. And they begin singing "Softly and Tenderly, Jesus is Calling." Awkwardly, at first. Then sweetly, as pride melts away into memory. Then, for two entire verses, the camera switches back and forth between the face of George and the face of

Madeleine (his wife), as she realizes ... for the first time ... who she has really married and what this place really means.

But I know what a place like this really means. Thirty-five years ago (on a Friday afternoon in June), I walked into this building hot, tired and sweaty, lugging yet one more box of books into my new office. Audrey Bueltemann, who was hovering near the kitchen, waiting for an appliance repair contractor said, "You must be the Sears Man."

Well, I wasn't. And I told her who I was. Whereupon she looked me up, down and sidewise, and said, "Oh." Her voice didn't sound very enthusiastic. But that's what happens when you fail to meet a matriarch's expectations.

Twenty-two years ago ... older ... grayer ... yet much better dressed ... I walked out of this building early on a June afternoon ... no evidence of sweat ... but with more than a few visible tears. Knowing that I was a far better person for the 13 years I spent here, along with realizing that they had just come to an end.

Later that evening, Freddy Timpner called to rehash the morning. And he said, "I don't know whether you felt it or not, but there sure was a lot of love in that place." I told him I felt it. Because there was. Still is.

This place. Your place. My place. God's place. Our place. Now let's finish the song.

Nardin Park United Methodist Church
Farmington Hill, Michigan
February 15, 2015

20

That'll Preach

Scripture: Isaiah 52:7-9 and Romans 10:14-17

With this sermon, my collection comes to an end. Just as with this sermon, my 12 years at in Birmingham came to an end.

To a roomful of preachers and preacher wannabes, a cherished colleague began anecdotally:

> *One of the good things that I got out of my ministry*
> *in Texas was a delightful story about a certain Mexican*
> *bank robber by the name of Juan Rodriguez, who*
> *operated along the Texas border around the turn of the*
> *century. He was so successful in his forays that the Texas*
> *Rangers put a whole extra posse along the Rio Grande to*
> *try and stop him. Sure enough, late one afternoon, one*

of these special Rangers saw Juan stealthily slipping across the river and trailed him at a discreet distance as he returned to his home village. He watched as Juan mingled with the people in the square around the town well and then went into his favorite cantina to relax. The Ranger slipped in and managed to get the drop on Juan. With a pistol to his head, he said, "I know who you are, Juan Rodriguez, and I have come to get back all the money you have stolen from the banks in Texas. Unless you give it to me, I am going to blow your brains out." There was one fatal difficulty, however. Juan did not speak English, and the Texas Ranger was not versed in Spanish. There they were, two adults at an utter verbal impasse.

But about that time, an enterprising eavesdropper came up and said, "I am bilingual. Do you want me to act as translator?" The Ranger nodded, and he proceeded to put the words of the Ranger into terms that Juan could understand. Nervously, Juan answered back: "Tell the big Texas Ranger that I have not spent a cent of the money. If he will go to the town well, face north, count down seven stones, he will find a loose one. Pull it out, and all the money is behind there. Please tell him quickly." The little translator got a solemn look on his face and said to the Ranger in perfect English: "Juan

Rodriguez is a brave man. He says he is ready to die."

From which I draw a pair of conclusions. First, what we don't know can hurt us. Second, when life and death are matters of language, you had better be able to trust your translator.

Which interests me more than a little, given that I have spent the last forty years of my life in the language and translation business. You have heard me say that most of us come to life carrying some sort of toolbox. But when I open mine, I find no hammers, heat thermometers or heart catheters. Neither do I find any slide rules or stethoscopes. Just words. Only words. Nothing but words. "Talk is cheap," some say. But it's put bread on my table ... and bread-eaters at the Lord's table.

To be sure, ministry is more than words. Much more than words. But I didn't know that when I was starting out. Because I don't remember having been called into ministry. I was still in high school when I went before my denomination's Board of Ministerial Training and Qualifications for the very first time. And nobody sitting around that table asked about my "call to ministry." Instead, they asked me to describe my "call to preach." Then they gave me a list of books to read so that upon completing them, I could be granted a License to Preach.

Today, all the nomenclature has changed. Nobody is asked about a "call to preach" anymore. Which, in a very small way ... but maybe not so small a way … contributes to a mindset that says preaching is not all that important anymore. But if that be true, why does preaching rise to the top of so many search committees' wish lists? And why does an unwillingness to prepare sermons diligently and deliver them adequately saddle so many careers to a lifetime of mediocrity?

Preaching …

Is it easy?

No, it's harder than ever.

Are congregational expectations lower?

No, they're higher than ever.

Are listeners patient, tolerant and forgiving?

No, they're more demanding than ever.

Why is that?

Because the need for a word, both timely and truthful, is greater than ever.

Virtually every other task of the ministry … from strumming four chords on my guitar so middle-schoolers could sing folk songs, to putting those same fingers in people's pockets so churches could build buildings … I learned as I went along. But from the very first time I stepped into a pulpit, I said to myself:

I must not fail at this.

I must bring the very best I have to this.

I must make the time ... not just hope to find
the time ... for this.

Because more than I will ever comprehend
is riding on this.

Over the flow of 2,080 Sundays, I have preached some bad sermons. But never once did I preach an under-prepared sermon. How long should preparation take? When I was in seminary, the rule of thumb was twenty hours (or one hour in the study for every minute in the pulpit). I confess I have never come close to that standard. But when you add up my reading, jotting, sketching, writing, rewriting and reviewing (the latter step requiring two hours on Saturday night after Kris goes to bed), the hours are never less than ten. And when you add re-dictating and proofreading for publication, you tack on two more for a total of twelve. Does any minister have that much time? No. Would preaching be better if more ministers took that much time? Yes.

So why don't they? Frankly, some are lazy. Others have different priorities. But more often than you would guess, many sell out before they start, fearing congregational indifference at best or congregational rejection at worst. One can almost hear those preachers say: "What if I put all that effort into it, and nothing comes from it? Or, worse yet, bad things come from it?" If a preacher is not moderately confident of success on the back end, it will curtail effort expended on the front end.

And then there's the matter of self-revelation. Good preachers begin with a text. But good preachers never hide behind their text. Meaning that preaching is incredibly self-exposing. When you take a Dale Carnegie course in public speaking (and would it surprise you to know that I have never taken a course in public speaking?), you are told to conquer your fear of the audience by picturing them naked. But what they never tell you in seminary is that one of the things that makes a sermon great is when the congregation is permitted to see the preacher naked.

But what a wonderful calling it is … challenge it is … opportunity it is … trust it is. When I started out, my fear was that I would drain my cup after three or four sermons. What I discovered was that mine is a cup-filling Lord … even a cup-overflowing Lord. Meaning that most Sundays I can preach out of the saucer. Today, my worry is different. I no longer worry about what I will do when the cup runs dry. Now I worry about what I will do with all the stuff that, thanks to the uncappable spring of the Spirit, keeps welling up inside me. I go through life seeing movies, reading books, holding conversations, eavesdropping on everyday life. Which leads me to say (ten or twenty times a day): "That'll preach." You and I look at the same stuff. You think it's interesting and may (or may not) remember to tell your spouse about it when you get home. I am already slotting it into a sermon. They tell me that George Buttrick (late of Madison Avenue Presbyterian Church in New York and Memorial Church at Harvard) wrote a new sermon every week of his life after his retirement. Not to keep his skill from declining. But because new material kept arriving.

But our material is not just random material. Our words are not just any words. And our sermons are more than simmering stockpots of chicken soup for the church-going soul. Instead, there's a point to all this talk … a life-changing, life-saving point.

Do you remember Scheherazade? Of course, you do. She was one of the wives of the Emperor of Persia. And Persia's emperor was a man who was convinced that all women were unfaithful. So he vowed he would marry a new wife each day, have his way with her at night, and would then have her executed the next morning. Which was a rather lethal problem. Except that Scheherazade was a very clever woman. Crafting a strategy to save her own neck, she ended up saving all the women of Persia. On her wedding night, she began to tell the emperor a tale that so fascinated him he decided to stay her execution for an additional night so he could hear the rest of the story. You know the outcome as well as I do. Scheherazade kept on talking, and so fascinated was the emperor that he listened to her tales for one thousand and one Arabian nights, after which he was sufficiently convinced of her fidelity that he made her his own.

Don't you see? Some stories are the thread upon which life itself depends. And the story "of Jesus and his love" is the one we preachers put forth as a means of offering the world a stay of execution. Still, as a story, it needs people who can tell it. "How shall they hear without preachers?" ponders Paul. By which he means people who fire the gospel story in the crucible of their lives and are not afraid to go public, Sunday after Sunday, to reveal the burn marks.

Bill Ritter's final sermon at
Birmingham First United Methodist Church, 2005

Preaching lives in the church when the gospel lives in the preacher. In a little letter called I Peter, Christians are told they should be prepared ... at the drop of a hat ... to defend the hope that is in them. Which suggests three things.

• That Christians will be ready.

• That Christians will be verbal.

• And that Christians will have hope in them that is so obvious that others will spot it, ask about it, and expect a reasonable explanation for it.

If I have heard it once in the last few weeks, I have heard it (quite literally) a hundred times. "Thanks," you have said, "for sharing so openly, honestly and personally with us." Which I have done, not accidentally, but intentionally. I am told by Eugene Peterson that it was once the fashion in Bohemia (no wonder I like the Czech Republic) to build pulpits in the form of upright whales. In order to take his or her place for delivery, the preacher was forced to enter the interior of the pulpit at the whale's tail, climb an upright ladder through the whale's belly, and then come into the whale's mouth to speak the word.

I have always wanted a pulpit like that. Not because I see myself as the mirror image of Jonah, but because I believe the best preaching occurs after the preacher has come through a dark and confining place, survived the experience of being lost at sea, or been nearly swallowed by forces bigger than life itself. My favorite definition of what it means to script words for a living came courtesy of the late sportswriter, Red Smith, who is alleged to have said: "Writing a daily column is really quite simple. All you have to do is sit down at the typewriter and open a vein." That's how I feel about sermons. One has to cut and bleed over them before they're done. As Harry Emerson Fosdick wrote in 1928:

"Nothing can make preaching easy. At best it means drenching a congregation with ones' lifeblood."

Hopefully, you have heard that in my preaching and have been transfused when blood was low and leaking. Over the years, some of you have had reasons to disagree with me about theology, philosophy, spirituality or worldly strategy. But if you have not seen in me evidence of the faith preached by me, then one of us has failed miserably, causing my sermons to misfire tragically. Because, in the words of the beloved hymn we shall soon sing, I wouldn't love to tell the story if it hadn't already done so much for me. "And that is just the reason I tell it now to thee."

One of you wrote: "I don't understand why you and your ministry represent security to me. But they do." Well, I don't understand that, either. But it may have something to do with the fact that I have never taken you where I haven't already been, or sold you something I haven't already bought. It is well with my soul. And "wellness of soul" is not something you can fake.

•••••••

Now it is time to move along so others can preach and bleed a bit. I can't begin to tell you how much like home this is, and how much like family you are. To a degree, every marriage of a Methodist preacher to a Methodist congregation is a forced marriage … at least an arranged marriage. But in this case, Bishop Ott, father really did know best. Infatuation was almost immediate. But our bonding came in the wake of tragedy, eleven months later. That bond remains ... can't help but remain ... and is virtually certain to remain. Retirement is not divorce. No one is asking us to love each other less. But our hearts are wider than we think, enabling us to make room for more than we think ... some of whom will soon arrive wearing nametags that say "Jack" and "Judy." Woo them, too. For when it comes to marrying ministry, you are allowed to commit bigamy.

Now it really is time to go. But let me route us by way of Columbus, Ohio where I once served as a seminary trustee. Picture Graduation Saturday in mid-May. See the faculty, students, family members, and friends seated on folding chairs in the great, green, grassy quadrangle facing the pillars of the library. Now watch as a scared-stiff student body president steps to the podium, having been chosen to speak a final word on behalf of the graduating seniors. Peering at this assemblage of dignitaries, classmates, and friends, he runs the gamut of things that nervous speakers do. He plays with his hair. He plays with his tie. He plays with his notes. He plays with the microphone. He sighs ... coughs ... clears his throat ... and says:

> *The chairs in which we sit are not the chairs of the prophets and the apostles.*

> *The chairs in which we sit are not the chairs at the left hand of power or the right hand of glory.*

The chairs in which we sit are not the chairs of the last, or even the next-to-last, judgment.

The chairs in which we sit are the property of the Greater Columbus Ohio Rent-All Society.

Which they were, of course. As are all chairs. Rented, I mean. No occupancy is permanent. Seminary is a rented chair. Ministry is a rented chair. Life, itself, is a rented chair. But how good this one felt. And how good this one fit. And for that, I thank you. Kris thanks you. Julie and Jared thank you. We will never forget you. And we will always care.

First United Methodist Church
Birmingham, Michigan
June 19, 2005

Note: The "Chairs In Which We Sit" lines also appear in a previous message. While the usages were similar, each was tailored to fit a different audience.

Permission vs Forgiveness

Other Books by William A. Ritter

Take The Dimness of My Soul Away:
healing after a loved one's suicide

In 1994 William Ritter's adult son committed suicide, sending Ritter and his family on a journey no family wants to take. Part of Ritter's own process of healing the loss of his son was to preach about it occasionally from the pulpit. This book is a collection of the sermons he preached, the first one just three weeks after his son's death, and the final one nine years later. Through them, we get a glimpse of a father and a family struggling honestly with their pain and gradually - over the years - coming to grips with their loss. Take the Dimness of My Soul Away will be a welcome companion to anyone who has lost a loved one to suicide, as well as to pastors and counselors who work with those who are grieving. Ritter offers no easy solutions, no rosy pictures, and no silver linings, but speaks honestly instead about the difficult emotions and confusion of this kind of loss, and ultimately, about a sense of hopefulness for the survivors of suicide.

Morehouse Publishing 2004 (ISBNo819221049)

More PRAISE ...

"Ritter" as some call him, is genuine, authentic, thoughtful, and is truly one of those people you only have the opportunity in life to come across once. He and his stories are one of the most treasured things that I have experienced in my 57 years on this planet. He is a theologian, a remarkable individual, an academic, storyteller, leader, preacher, parent, grandfather ("Boppa"), husband (To Kris "Neena"), and a friend to all that have crossed paths with him. His wife Kris who went to school with one of my brothers is also a talented and remarkable person who compliments Bill in every way with her wit, grace, intelligence, and grounding in many of the stories you are about to read.   I am truly honored and privileged to call the Ritter's friends and I have used sections of these stories in my day-to-day conversations, because life is a *"people business"* and these stories are reflections of all of us. Dr. Ritter's gift to us tugs on our heartstrings. As you read you think he is talking directly to you when he opens up emotionally in his authentic way from his own life's journey. Read up, take it all in, enjoy this collection now and share with the next generation ... because all these stores will preach in your world, too. PEACE!

Brian P. Turnbull
Men's Club President-FUMC Northville and Auto Industry Consultant